Know Thyself

The Stress Release Programme

Know Thyself

The Stress Release Programme

Dr Craig Hassed

MICHELLE ANDERSON PUBLISHING

This book is dedicated to the great traditions of wisdom across cultures and throughout history and to the teachers and writers who have made this wisdom so accessible to us. It is also dedicated to those who express wisdom and compassion in the way they live their lives. Gratitude is given for the open-mindedness, encouragement and support of Monash University, the RACGP and the people who have helped me in my professional life such as Neil Carson, John Murtagh, Leon Piterman, Lyn Clearihan, Merilyn Liddell, Steven Sommer and many others with whom I have worked. Thanks and encouragement is given to the thoughtful and interested medical students who are our future doctors, without whom a teacher is both uninspired and redundant. Last but not least it is dedicated to my parents, Bob and Shirley, and to my wife, Deirdre, for all they have selflessly given over my lifetime.

First published in Australia 2002
by Michelle Anderson Publishing Pty Ltd
PO Box 6032, Chapel Street North
South Yarra, Melbourne 3141 Australia
Tel: 03 9826 9028
Fax: 03 9826 8552
Email: mapubl@bigpond.net.au
www.michelleandersonpublishing.com

Cover design: Deborah Snibson Modern Art Production Group
Typeset by Midland Typesetters, Maryborough
Printed in Australia by McPhersons Printing, Maryborough

National Library of Australia Cataloguing-in-Publication data

Hassed, Craig.
Know thyself : the stress release programme

Bibliography.
ISBN 0 85572 336 X

1. Stress management. I. Title

155.9042

Contents

Foreword

Stress has become such an inseparable part of modern life that we have almost forgotten what it is like to live without it. In fact, it has almost become an obligation. Rightly or wrongly, it has become a catch-word to cover all manner of experiences. When needed, stress can be helpful but when prolonged and excessive it can be the source of much physical and psychological illness.

This book and the practices it outlines are not just meant for those with extreme stress-related problems. It is for everyday people (whoever they are) leading everyday lives (whatever that is). It was self-evident to me in my youth that there was much I did not understand about myself and that I had a lot to learn with respect to leading a fulfilling and productive life. I found that others, like myself, also needed to learn how to recognise and deal with our stress in a far more constructive and practical way. It was in this context that I found the principles of mindfulness and the practice of meditation enormously helpful and applicable. They were at the same time undeniably simple and yet enormously profound.

Many professionals such as doctors, psychologists and coun-sellors may find this program a sound basis upon which to extend their own professional skills. It is important, however, that before using the principles and practices of mindfulness with others one has used them consistently oneself. Then and only then can the teaching be passed on through experience and not just theory.

Mindfulness is most sensibly used in a preventive way and to help us cope effectively with demanding and busy lives. It is a simple and gentle way of dealing with smaller problems before they become larger ones, or as an adjunct for dealing with more major issues. If major issues do ensue then it would be wise to use the mindfulness approach in conjunction with professional counselling and/or medication as required.

This book is a culmination of many years of experience, practise and teaching in personal and professional stress man-agement. It covers the Mindfulness-based Stress Release Program (SRP), which has been authored by myself and run at the Royal Australian College of General Practitioners, through Monash University undergraduate and postgraduate medical training, and for various professional and lay audiences since 1991.

The SRP is process-oriented, not theoretical. You can simply read the book from cover to cover but far better than that would be to perform the tasks and practices week by week. This will allow them to sink in. Examine them carefully by testing them out in the context of your own experience. Do not accept anything unquestioningly. The principles of mindfulness in one sense are universal, but it is up to each individual to apply them to their particular situation in life. A number of the key princi-ples will be emphasised on more than one occasion. It is hoped that you will see this as reinforcement, rather than repetition.

The mindfulness approach is both very new and very old. Much of the content goes back thousands of years, but it is finding a new expression and application in contemporary life. An increasing amount of research is confirming this in a variety of settings for issues concerning both physical and mental health. Some of this research on mindfulness will be referred to later along with some studies on other forms of meditation. I hope you find it as helpful in your life as I have in mine.

Stress and stress management

Introduction

Have you ever had an anxious or fearful thought? Have you ever found it difficult to get your attention off unhelpful patterns of thought and on to something more useful or constructive? Have you ever found that your mind wanders even when you would rather it didn't? Do you find that your life often feels like it is being lived under a cloud? Are you ever regretful about the past or apprehensive about the future? Do you sometimes feel that you are not making the best of your time, abilities and opportunities? Do you find it difficult to change behaviour even when you want to? Well, perhaps mindfulness might be relevant for you.

Mindfulness is a simple but effective way of getting to know ourselves better. It can help us to shed a little more light on our lives and our reactions to the people and events in our lives. Put another way, it is learning to live more consciously. It is only when we are more conscious of what is going on around and within us that we can even begin to do something constructive about it. Mindfulness concepts and practices, although far from new, are finding an increasing relevance and application in the modern and highly demanding world we live in.

Know Thyself

Inscribed over the entrance to the Temple at Delphi in ancient Greece were the words, 'Know Thyself'. This was echoed by Socrates, the wisest of the ancient Greek philosophers when he said, 'The unexamined life is not worth living.' He also said, 'Self-knowledge would certainly be maintained by me to be the very essence of knowledge.'

The notion that awareness, self-knowledge and happiness are inextricably linked has arisen from many centuries of astute observation of the human condition. It has also been echoed in the East but, of course, if something is a universal principle then divisions between East and West will be largely irrelevant.

> **'The wise man guards his mindfulness as his greatest treasure.'**
> —*Dhammapada*

Socrates was aware then, as we are now, that our main goal in our quest for happiness is self-understanding through awareness and observation. It is a prerequisite for being free as well as dealing effectively with the stresses and anxieties of daily life.

> **'Eternal vigilance is the price of liberty.'**
> —*John Curran*

A lack of awareness and an unwillingness to examine ourselves is a recipe for repeating old mistakes. Truly may it be said, ignorance is not bliss. Self-examination is about examining our beliefs, opinions, habits, reactions and attitudes—not just for the sake of it, but because this is where we will find the source of much of our stress and anxiety. Many of the false beliefs and opinions, many of the unhelpful habits and reactions are at best superfluous and at worst harmful. Those beliefs, opinions, habits and reactions which we do find to be useful will be affirmed, but the unhelpful ones need to be seen and discarded.

What is stress?

Stress is a commonly used term that covers a wide range of human experiences. Some people describe it as a 'perceived inability to cope', others as when 'demands exceed means'. However we define it, it is the experience of stress on our minds and bodies which is of immediate relevance to us.

The fight or flight response

We often use the word 'stress' to describe the physical effects associated with anxiety or fear. These well-recognised effects include muscle tension, tremulousness, clamminess and rapid heartbeat. They are manifestations of what we call the 'fight or flight response'. When they become chronic or extreme they can lead to tiredness and many other stress-related symptoms, or even a complete inability to function.

The stress response is mediated by the autonomic nervous system (ANS) of the body. The ANS has the role of moderating various functions ranging from heart rate and blood flow to digestion and sexual response. It is one of the ways in which mental and emotional states can produce wide-ranging effects on health and function. Hence we will have noticed that when we are in a situation which we see as a stressful or threatening we will also notice related symptoms over which we seem to have little control, such as our heart thumping, butterflies in the stomach or an inability to become aroused. In some situations such sensations can become extreme and struggling with them in an endeavour to gain the control which we seem to have lost only seems to accentuate them. One of the tricks, which we will come to later, is to learn not to struggle but to flow with such sensations.

> **Paradox number 1: Self-control comes with conscious relaxation, not tension. It is a 'letting go' rather than a 'holding on.'**

The ANS is made up of two parts, the sympathetic nervous system (SNS) and the parasympathetic nervous system (PNS). The former is associated with activation, as in when we need to respond to a threatening event, and the latter with those functions which take place during times of calm. In a manner of speaking, they are like the Yin and the Yang of the body. The stress reaction that we call the fight or flight response is associated with pressure, demands, anxiety or fear. It is an activation largely of the SNS in response to a perceived threat. The name is apt, as it intimates that if we came face to face with a tiger we might need to quickly fight it or run from it. It is like a burst of turbo-charged energy mediated through adrenaline and many other chemicals. The fight or flight response has an important role in our lives. Without switching it on *when necessary*, we would not survive very long as individuals or as a species. The unfortunate thing is that we often switch this response on unnecessarily.

What switches on this physical series of events? It is the state of mind—in particular the emotions. Stress is a word also used to describe psychological, emotional and existential states like confusion, distractibility, forgetfulness, worry, fear, anger, frustration, aimlessness, despondency and depression. Over the course of a day or a year we can cycle through a variety of these states as mind and body intimately communicate with each other. Therefore, one cannot take the label 'stress' at face value without exploring fully what a person means by it.

Stress and depression are well known to be connected.

Western societies are observing similar increases in rates of depression and suicide. Some predictions estimate that depression may be the major cause of debilitation and illness within a few decades. Panic attacks and anxiety are also becoming far more common. Much research has gone into researching the effects of stress in recent years.[1,2] Whether real or perceived, evidence suggests that the stress of modern life is increasing at an alarming rate; 45% over the last 30 years in some surveys.[3] This could be explained by both increased awareness of stress and also more stressful and busy lives. The rapid increase in the amount of social change, job insecurity, the speed of life, competitiveness and many other factors probably all contribute. Strangely, having too little to do, such as is the case with unemployment, can be just as stressful and demoralising as having too much to do although it might express itself in a different way to stress caused by having too many demands.

However stress is experienced, one of its most common manifestations is the use or overuse of sedatives and antidepressants. Even though in selected situations these can play a helpful role, are they the only option? Is this really what nature intended? Certainly there are biochemical changes in the brain associated with these various emotional states, but the issue is whether they are being driven by the thoughts behind them. This is a hotly debated issue by researchers and clinicians. It has an influence over whether one takes a largely pharmaceutical approach to such problems or a more holistic one. The issue will not be dealt with at length here. For now we will keep our discussions practical.

Surveys such as the ones referred to above measure people's responses to what they perceive as stressful life events. These events can include anything, but the more extreme ones tend to be major events like the death of a spouse, losing a job, divorce and separation, legal problems or imprisonment. Minor stressors can include things which are less extreme like deadlines, traffic, daily conflicts with people and so on. A stressful life can be one filled with many minor stressors or a few major ones, but the important thing is that, firstly, chronic stress or the accumulation of a number of minor stresses is a contributor to, or direct cause of, many illnesses and, secondly, it impairs our relationships and enjoyment of life.

Figures indicating that stress is increasing can paint a negative picture and need to be considered with care. They do not tell the whole picture, for there is a lot that a person can do to help themselves. A superficial reading of these rating scales of life stress do not take into account the fact that the stress is far less dependent on the actual event as it is on how the person *sees* and *responds* to the event. We will examine this in far greater detail, because this is one of the main avenues for dealing with stress mindfully. With a little care and attention we can literally change the way we perceive and respond to stressful life-events.

On one level the fight or flight response is a natural, necessary and appropriate physiological response to an exceptional situation. For example, if one is about to be bitten by a snake or be run over by a truck then one may need to respond quickly to get out of the way. This response, based on a clearly perceived threat, is encoded into our physiology to *preserve life* by allowing the body to respond to dangerous situations. Nature does not do things by chance or without purpose. If we did not have that response carefully coded into our systems we would be soon extinct as a species. When the threat is over the physiology will return to rest if the mind leaves the event in the past and moves on.

The anticipation of an event or the replaying of an event in the mind, however, can reproduce the stress response even though the event may never happen or is over. Winston Churchill must have known something about dealing with stress and also about the mind's ability to create stress when he said, 'When I look back on all these worries I remember the story of the old man who said on his death-bed that he had had a lot of troubles in his life, most of which never happened.'

The total fabrication or the replaying of an event in the mind can reproduce the stress response again and again. The response, over time, can become conditioned or habitual. The longer this goes on the more work and patience it may take to un-condition the response. In the most extreme cases this replaying can lead to what is called 'post-traumatic stress disorder'. It is as if the situation and response has been 'burned' into the memory emotionally and also the into biochemistry of the brain. In fact, it is thought that the level of stress and emotion at the time of an event can have a significant effect on determining how the event will be recalled. With care, patience and perseverance, this can be changed.

Is stress of any use?

Stress and performance

Those acquainted with the 'stress–performance curve' (see Fig. 1, below) will know that stress is often valued as a means of motivation. Indeed, it can lift us out of procrastination and inertia to a level of improved performance. This strategy works to an extent, but if stress is allowed to build it can easily lead to diminished performance and burnout. This has become an all too common occurrence.

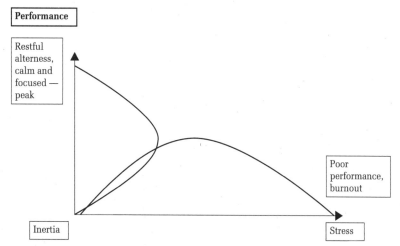

Fig. 1: Stress–performance curve

Peak and sustainable performance, on the other hand, is cultivated through a calm and focused state of mind, sometimes called restful alertness or mindfulness. It means learning to focus our attention and energy effectively while releasing the unnecessary and inhibiting effect of tension. As a result performance improves, but it is accompanied by a sense of peacefulness and wellbeing. Sometimes such a state of peak performance is called 'the zone' in athletic circles. This will be discussed more fully in the later section on mindfulness, but it might be useful to hear one athlete's description of a moment in the zone and functioning at her peak. Note the aspects of connectedness with what she is doing (mindfulness), peacefulness and freedom from fear about the outcome.

'I can hear the noise of the water flowing around me when I get the rhythm right. It's a really relaxing feeling to be able to swim really fast and it feels so easy, like it's effortless.'
—*Samantha Riley*: one time swimming world record holder

Such observations, which will be recognised by amateur athletes as well as professional ones, tend to go against our usual assumptions about the relationship between performance and relaxation. There is a form of relaxation that is indeed associated with inertia and lethargy as you will see on the diagram, but there is another option when we get to the crest of the stress–performance curve, which does not involve dropping of performance or burning out. This is worth cultivating.

One of the unfortunate assumptions that many people make about relaxation is that it is associated with poor performance or not caring about things. This is true of the ways of relaxation that are associated with inertia and procrastination, but it is not true for a mindful and reasonable approach to dealing with unwanted and unproductive tension and the waste of energy that comes in its wake. Peak and sustainable performance is cultivated through a calm, conscious and focused state of mind. It means four things in relation to energy.

1. Making better use of our energy by learning to focus our attention and energy more effectively.
2. Conserving energy by releasing the unnecessary, inhibiting and wasteful effect of tension.
3. Being able to replenish energy by being better able to 'refuel' when we need to.
4. Finding new reserves of energy by being able to have access to energy that was not available before.

Although a level of stress can be associated with motivation, and although the 'fight or flight' response can be entirely necessary in extreme situations, the vast majority of stress experienced in daily life is not appropriate, productive or helpful. The unnecessary and excessive switching on of the stress response, which we might call inappropriate stress, though common, is not healthy and does not help us to cope with demands. In fact it does quite the opposite.

Stress and adversity

There is another way in which stress can be helpful. It can wake us up. It would be entirely more sensible to find a gentler way to wake up, but nevertheless the emotional pain associated with stress can be useful. If used with care, stress and adversity can teach us much about ourselves and, in a strange sort of way, bring out the best in us. In this way many people find that the most stressful life events, sometimes even as extreme as getting cancer, can bring out a strength that we did not know we had.

> 'This is not flattery: these are counsellors
> That feelingly persuade me what I am.
> Sweet are the uses of adversity,
> Which like the toad, ugly and venomous,
> Wears a precious jewel in its head.'
> —*Shakespeare:* As You Like It, *ii. 1*

> **Paradox 2: What is pleasant or easy is not always what is best for us and what is difficult or uncomfortable is not always bad for us.**

It is very much like physical pain; it is there for a good reason. It is there to show us that some injury has taken place and that it needs some attention to put it right. It would not be reasonable if we had our hand on a hotplate to just ask someone to take the pain away with a strong pain-killer. It would be better to pay attention to what is happening and to make the necessary adjustment; in this case take the hand off the hotplate. Stress and other forms of emotional pain are very similar. The very fact that we are experiencing them suggests to us that we need to have a look at the thought patterns behind them.

The thinking behind the stress

It does not take a lot of observation to notice the character of thought when the mind is stressed. Here the mind is generally agitated and unfocussed. One can, and usually does, become overwhelmed with imaginings, projections and anticipation, which are given a reality they do not deserve. Rather than a highly conscious and aware state this is the opposite. Examples might include projecting fears into the future about exams or interviews, catastrophising about upcoming events and habitually recreating past anxieties and conflicts. Here the stressors are in the mind, not in reality. The body, however, receiving its instructions from the command centre, the mind, will faithfully reproduce the stress response until it is told to stop, regardless of whether the stressor is real or imagined. If one imagines a rope to be a snake the body will react to the perception, not the reality.

Even events that are actually happening may or may not

cause stress depending on what the mind thinks about them. Events are just events unless our minds label and interpret them as stressful and threatening. As Shakespeare so aptly said, 'There is nothing either good or bad but thinking makes it so.'

If stress arises in response to a threat, then what is being threatened when we notice stress arising? A tiger about to pounce on us is an obvious threat to the physical body. But fear and stress will be elicited by a threat to 'self', whatever we take 'self' to be. If we take self as the body then we feel threatened if the body is threatened. Although such fears are nearly always exaggerated, this response nevertheless has an important role for protection of the body. But there is far more to us than the body.

The more common threat to self that causes us stress, however, is not a threat to the body but rather a threat to the *idea* of self, sometimes called the small self or 'ego'. The word 'idea' is not used unadvisedly because with a little reflection we soon find that this ego-centred notion of self is a collection of ideas. It is like an image we have of ourselves that is constituted by a bundle of ideas, opinions, roles, habits, desires, aversions and the rest. It is often a type of false-self that we construct, believe, defend and justify but—and this is the interesting thing—we can examine it. What is looking and what is being looked at? The very fact that we can study and observe it suggests to us that there is another Self doing the looking. This 'conscious Self' is often referred to as the central or 'big Self' and so is sometimes spelt with a capital letter. The lesser self which is observable is often referred to as the ego and so is generally spelt with a small s. To quote Shakespeare again, 'To thine own self be true and it must follow, as the night the day, thou cans't not then be false to any man.'

We may have noticed that when we look at ourselves with some level of objectivity in this way we often find that many of the things that we take so seriously start to appear a little comic. This, of course, is one of the essential features of comedy. It is a way of standing back from ourselves and seeing what strange creatures we often are.

If we take our self to be our opinions, for example, then when one of our opinions gets challenged we feel challenged. It is not seen as just an opportunity to discuss the merits of differing points of view but rather as a threat to 'me' and all the related ideas I have about myself, like 'I am well informed', 'I am intelligent', 'I am right', and so on. Understandably, anger, attack and defence arise quite readily. Of course, if we were more objective about the opinion then such situations would not be so threatening and the discussion could be far more focused and reasonable. If, on examination, the opinion has merit then we can retain it. If it has no merit we can thankfully discard it and be better off, but if the discussion takes place from a more ego-centred point of view then such unbiased discussion is an impossibility.

Furthermore, if we totally identify ourselves with a certain role, like being a doctor, father or mother, then if that role is criticised—rightly or wrongly—the criticism feels intensely personal. Experiencing such an intense personal feeling is a fair indication that a level of ego is involved. If I have a picture of myself as being intelligent or generous or honest then any challenge to that perception is seen as a direct threat, even though there might be all the evidence in the world that we are not always intelligent, generous or honest. When one of our habitual ways of doing things gets upset then rather than being seen as an opportunity for a little creativity it is seen as something threatening and disorientating. We can see that our sense of 'I' gets associated with many different things.

One of the things that happens when the ego gets involved in our activities is that objectivity and clarity gets sacrificed and with them goes effective action. It gets harder and harder to be able to respond to events on their merits and if we are not able to respond appropriately then we are not able to act responsibly because, despite all the connotations we commonly attach to responsibility, it simply means 'ability to respond'. If one were able to drop the ego then one might surprisingly find that most of the threats would dissolve and with them the fear, anger, frustration or grief which inevitably accompanies them. Indeed, having dropped the ego there is still an issue to deal with, a decision to make, or a question to resolve. That does not go away. What does go away is the stress and agitation associated with it. We start to respond from a different place.

Thus, the mind has a key role in eliciting the stress response through its functions of perception, cognition, interpretation, and conditioning. Healthy and unhealthy patterns of behaviour are to some extent inherited and to some extent learned.

In a manner of speaking, learned patterns of coping and personality styles are possibly more important than a situation itself in determining how much stress we experience. One can readily see how important techniques such as meditation, mindfulness, cognitive-behaviour therapy (CBT) and rational-emotive therapy (RET) are in helping us to reverse the effects of this inappropriate stress by attacking it at its cause: inappropriate thought.

Acknowledging this fact empowers us to be more proactive and understand ourselves better by taking conscious charge of these responses. Any response to stress that merely apportions blame to the environment will be of very limited success as it ignores the most important element in the process: the person responding to the environment. This, of course, does not preclude the fact that a more conscious and focused response to daily events may be exactly what is required. If there really is a snake in the vicinity then evasive action may be needed. Furthermore, one must be careful that in the acknowledgement of the role of the individual in generating their own stress, and all that comes with it, it is important to not encourage a process of self-blame. Responsibility is much more about fostering a healthy ability to respond than it is about blame or recrimination. Learn by all means, but move on.

Paradox 3: Self-blame will slow the process of self-development, not speed it.

Is dealing with stress a complicated process?

Yes and no. Stress is certainly a complicated state but many of the remedies are simple. There is a common perception that dealing with stress-related issues requires discomfort and in-depth psychoanalysis. In the great majority of cases this need not be so, but it does require paying attention to healthy and unhealthy ways of using the mind. A more positive way to look at it is to acknowledge that we have the ability to harm or help ourselves and to become aware—without criticism—of negative coping styles and reactions and then, like a gardener, to carefully weed them out while cultivating the more positive ones. This way empowers us to understand ourselves better and take charge of our responses. Learning and practising some simple exercises and tasks is feasible so that we can adapt them to our individual needs.

'Stress management' is a familiar term. It is no longer frowned upon to learn how to manage stress better, and sometimes one wonders whether there is almost an unspoken obligation for people to be stressed, particularly in the workplace. It is almost as if there is an assumption that 'if you're not stressed then you couldn't possibly be working hard enough'.

Within all this stress and striving there is the natural and universal human search for true fulfilment, peace and happiness. When we look at everything going on in the world, it is all aimed at pursuing happiness and avoiding unhappiness. Sadly, if we do not know ourselves or where our happiness lies then our actions are often misdirected. As a result what was meant to produce happiness often leads to the exact opposite, not just for ourselves but also for those around us. In its largest sense, stress management is simply about facilitating the natural search for true and lasting fulfilment, peace and happiness. The principles and goals are simple, but the obstacles can appear complicated.

The relationship between consciousness, mind and body

This relationship will not be discussed in detail here, but it is important to appreciate the principle. There is a vast body of scientific research in the field described as Mind-Body Medicine and its offspring, Psychoneuroimmunology. The language and science is complicated, but the principle is simple and was summed up by Hippocrates when he said, 'The human being can only be understood as a whole.'

The human organism works as a whole. Broadly speaking, there are three aspects to our being.

1. The consciousness
2. The mind, including the thoughts and emotions (the mental)
3. The body (the physical)

The consciousness, like the power source, enlivens the thoughts and emotions of the mind and this in turn affects the physical aspects: the physiology, biochemistry and behaviour of the body. If we give our consciousness to a thought it is like plugging it into that power-source. It is no small matter what we choose to direct consciousness towards, and this choice is exercised by reason or the lack of it. This relationship is often described by the use of analogy in philosophical and literary writings. For example, consciousness, which is often associated with the spiritual, is often represented as light and the body as shadow.

> 'For in and out, above, about, below
> 'Tis nothing but a magic shadow show,
> Played in a box whose candle is the sun,
> Round which we phantom figures come and go.'
> —*Omar Khayyam,* The Rubaiyat of Omar Khayyam

'Life's but a walking shadow,
A poor player that struts and frets his hour upon the stage and
then is heard no more. It is a tale, told by an idiot, full of
sound and fury, signifying nothing.'
—*Shakespeare* Macbeth

The body is also often represented as a vehicle and the mind as
the driver.

'Self rides in the chariot of the body,
Intellect the firm footed charioteer,
Discursive mind the reins,
Senses are the horses,
Objects of desire the roads.
When self is joined to body, mind, sense, none but he enjoys.'
—*Upanishads*

The thoughts and emotions that go through the mind obviously
not only affect the body directly, but also our lifestyle, relationships and work. When the thoughts and emotions are in harmony
then optimal health is possible, but when thoughts and emotions
are ill at ease then poor health usually results sooner or later, and
recovery is much more difficult. To adequately treat most medical
conditions we need to at least be mindful of this holistic and
dynamic relationship between consciousness, mind and body.
Stress, and poor mental health in general, is being recognised as
a major contributor to physical illness. It can also place an
enormous burden upon the individual and his/her workplace,
family and community. It may manifest itself in countless ways:

- the obvious presenting problem, for example, anxiety alone
  is one of the commonest reasons for patients presenting to
  doctors.
- one of the many physical ailments commonly associated
  with it, such as headaches, peptic ulcer or hypertension.

- a contributing factor to illnesses such as heart disease, cancer and infections through poor immunity.
- a result of a poorly adaptive behavioural response to coping with stress which includes:
  - unhealthy lifestyles such as smoking, alcohol and drug abuse.
  - social problems such as domestic violence, aggression, depression, poor work performance and avoidance behaviour.

There is an important, simple but very practical principle to appreciate. Attention fed to thoughts and emotions gives them 'their' power. It is a little like television ratings. If a pattern of thought is popular and getting a lot of viewer attention it will keep getting reruns. It does not matter at all what the inherent merits of the thoughts are. If the ratings go down, however, because there is little interest from the audience, then it will soon be taken off the air. We can learn to direct our attention as simply as that, although we may be working against a compulsive and habitual tendency to give attention to the same thought patterns again and again.

These thoughts power physical responses just as the thoughts of the driver affects a car's performance. The body is always reflecting what the mind is telling it. It is easy to see that conscious thoughts precede words and actions; what is sometimes less obvious is that unconscious or unobserved thoughts also lead to automatic physiological responses and actions. Importantly, it is well nigh impossible to make and maintain constructive lifestyle changes while we are stressed or depressed but conversely, when we deal with stress better or recover from depression we often find the motivation and strength to make healthy lifestyle change arises quite spontaneously.

Just as we cannot look at the functioning of any one part of the body in isolation from other parts, we cannot divide a person's intellectual, social and emotional responses into isolated compartments. Our state of mind tends to effect all aspects of our lives. The insidious thing about stress is that it can be well established without our being greatly aware of it, and it often takes a crisis before we as individuals or groups are motivated enough to take constructive steps to resolve it. Ignorance is not bliss, just as being unaware that the coronary arteries are blocked will not postpone a potential heart attack.

A professor was once asked, 'What is the country's greatest undoing, ignorance or apathy?' to which he replied, 'I don't know and I don't care.' Ignorance and apathy are two of stress' greatest allies. Although we cannot avoid stressful situations in daily living, we can increase our ability to cope constructively with them. This is what the SRP aims to do. It will gently but surely address this lack of awareness through mindfulness. For the purposes of the program which follows we will be dealing with the sort of stress that is part of the experience of most people in modern life. Although better coping strategies are important for those with more major psychiatric illnesses, it is not intended that this program be applied to psychosis or more serious psychiatric conditions. It is not that relaxation exercises and counselling may not help in such situations, but it may be more prudent to enlist the aid of individualised assessment by specialists in conjunction with appropriate medication where necessary.

Research data about the links between mind and body

'For this is the great error of our day in the treatment of the human body, that physicians separate the soul from the body.'
—*Plato*, Chamides

Psychological stress is increasingly being recognised by doctors as a major contributor to ill-health and yet we have tended to ignore the potential of using the mind to facilitate the healing process. That the mind has a powerful effect on the body is not only proven by anecdotal evidence. It is also the subject of an enormous body of scientific evidence in areas such as Mind-Body Medicine (MBM) and the best known sub-specialty of MBM called psychoneuroimmunology. The effects of psychological and emotional disharmony can be shown to have disruptive effects upon many facets of health, in particular physiological homoeostasis (the body's ability to balance and regulate its functions), immune function (our front-line defence against illness and external attack), the endocrine system (the hormones which communicate between organs and regulate function) and musculoskeletal function. In the future it is likely that scientific research will demonstrate that many physical conditions not previously linked with stress and poorly adapted responses to it, may be found to be significantly contributed to by psychosocial factors. Likewise there is growing evidence that restoration of psychological wellbeing and peace of mind has an enormously positive effect upon a person's ability to recover from and cope with illness, to deal effectively with work and relationships, and to solve problems. Encouragingly, the side-effects from effective stress management seem to be useful.

Interestingly, although physical illness issues are often the initial motivator for engaging in stress management, it is often the beneficial side-effects—being better able to deal with work and relationships or being better able to problem-solve—that keep us doing it. Although medication is sometimes required for significant emotional disturbance, it is unfortunate that the side-effects from this are not always useful, which is one of the major reasons why people are turning to natural alternatives in great numbers. In one study it was found that anxiety was one of the commonest reasons predicting why people searched outside the conventional medical system for their health care,[4] which is understandable considering that many people receive little more than drugs. People are reasonably looking for a far more holistic solution. Not only does an effective stress management plan have application for resolving problems, it is also useful for preventing them. Many of the less useful ways of adapting to stress have very deleterious side-effects.

It is beyond the brief of this book to give a detailed overview of the field of mind-body medicine. A summary of some of the main areas where meditation has been presently researched is given in the following two tables.

Acknowledging the intimate relationship between the mind and the body is important but, there are a few cautions also.

1. That stress can have a negative effect on virtually every medical condition does not mean that we can ignore the physical illness and the physical treatments which might help. These need to be used in conjunction. The mind can have a powerful effect on the body, but one should be cautious about the notion that one can 'wish away' illnesses.
2. Furthermore, it does not mean that we cannot assume that any symptoms which might have a basis in stress are due to stress only. There will always be a need for appropriate physical examination and the judicial use of tests where appropriate to identify physical illness.
3. Although the role of the mind is the central pillar of good health it does not mean that we can ignore the other pillars such as healthy diet, exercise, social support, balance of work and rest, and avoidance of toxins, including smoking and inappropriate use of drugs (prescribed or unprescribed).

The following tables list some of the research into the benefits of stress reduction and meditation. The list is by no means exhaustive.

Table 1: Physiological benefits of relaxation and stress reduction

- Marked decrease in oxygen consumption and metabolic rate well below that achieved in sleep, decrease in respiration rate and minute ventilation associated with greater efficiency and economy, and a lowering of catechol receptor sensitivity.[5,6,7]
- Reduction in blood pressure and heart rate.[8]
- Reduction in serum cholesterol, more than would be accounted for by diet alone, sharp increase in skin resistance (low skin resistance is an accurate marker of stress responses), decrease in blood lactate, associated with anaerobic metabolism which is high in stressful situations[9].
- Changes in EEG patterns associated with the state of restful alertness including an increase in alpha and theta waves and EEG coherence (coordination of EEG waves).[10]
- A reduction in epileptic seizure frequency.[11]
- Changes in neurotransmitter profile including high serotonin production as seen in recovery from depression.[12]
- A suggested selective increase in cerebral blood flow.[13]
- Reduction in cortisol levels.
- Reduced TSH and T3 levels.[14]
- Improved response time and reflexes.[15]
- Improvement in perceptiveness of hearing and other senses.[16]
- Improved immune function. For an immune system under-active due to chronic stress it is stimulated and for over-active immune systems such as in

auto-immune and inflammatory illnesses it seems to reduce its over-activity.[1,2]

- Increased calcium loss and osteoporosis is associated with high cortisol levels and depression.[17]
- Very beneficial as an adjunct to therapy for a variety of illnesses such as heart disease, cancer, chronic pain[18], asthma[19], diabetes[20] and many others.

Table 2: Psychological benefits of stress reduction

- Decreased anxiety.[21,22]
- More optimism, decreased depression as indicated by elevation of serotonin.[23,24]
- Greater self-awareness and self-actualisation.[25]
- Improved coping capabilities.[26]
- Happiness tends to be less conditional. Improved well-being and as an adjunct to psychotherapy.[27]
- Reduced reliance upon drugs, prescribed and non-prescribed, or alcohol.[28]
- Improved sleep[29]; more restful, less insomnia, and in time less sleep needed.
- Reduced aggression and criminal tendency.[30]
- Improved I.Q. and learning capabilities, including the aged and intellectually impaired.
- Greater efficiency and output and reduced stress at work.[31]
- Better time management.
- Improved concentration and memory.[32] [33]
- Reduction in personality disorders and ability to change undesired personality traits.[34]
- Stimulus reduction was the most effective known form of treatment for infantile colic.[35]

The Stress Release Program– mindfulness-based stress management

Obviously in-depth counselling is not always an option for many therapists and patients because of many practical reasons including cost, time and motivation, but learning and practising some simple exercises is feasible. Though the following principles and practices in the stress-release program are quite universal, we need to adapt them according to our individual needs.

Principles of the SRP

The Stress Release Program is an approach to stress management that utilises mindfulness and meditation. It is based upon the following simple principles.

- Our own skills of coping, insight and reflection are our best resource.
- We are only learning what we intuitively know but perhaps have forgotten.
- We set the agenda, goals and rate of progress; often we need to start with small problems and work up to larger ones as strength and confidence grow.
- Sincere effort and practise translate into more rapid progress.
- Self-motivation is all-important; one moves with the guidance and encouragement of the course notes or leader.
- Simplicity, not sophistication, is paramount.
- The SRP is a practical and not a theoretical course. The proof is in the pudding not the theory. It is based on:
  - Observation
  - Practice
  - Experience

How does the program adhere to these principles?

The steps involved in the program are simple and methodical.

1. Initially the aim is to provide education about stress and its effects, which you have already read about.
2. Next we learn some simple skills of relaxation, observation and personal growth based on mindfulness.
3. These skills are practised on a daily basis. With practical experience you transform theory into understanding.
4. The eight tasks are a natural extension of mindfulness exercises into our daily life. These are best practised one new task per week.
5. The skills and insights gained from this course will grow over time if we continue to apply the principles and practices.

The cornerstone of the program is regularly practising the mindfulness exercise, ideally twice a day. This will help to release both physical and mental tension, to focus attention more effectively and to channel energies more usefully. Many would call this a *relaxation exercise*, some would call it *attention focusing* and others would call it *a meditation exercise*. These are just different aspects of the same thing. The label is not so important as the need to practise it regularly and to see what we can learn from it. It is difficult to do any useful work in stress management unless we have a way of raising our awareness first. It should be emphasised, however, that the choice to practise this or any other exercise will always rest with yourself. Motivation comes best from our own insight and experience.

Running alongside this mindfulness exercise are the eight weekly tasks. Read the chapter for one new task at the beginning of each week and then reflect on it and practise it over that week. The practice will be summed up in the box at the end of the chapter on each task.

You might find it helpful to keep a journal and note down observations, experiences and questions as you go. If doing this course in a group with a counsellor it is very important to speak about what you are finding each week with regard to your observations, practise (or lack of it) and experiences. Our so-called failures are not really failures at all. They can be just as instructive as our so-called successes. Pay attention to all of it and ask questions about things you do not understand when you have the opportunity.

Many of the insights we gain will challenge long-held assumptions we have made about ourselves in terms of self-control, happiness, the world, our relationships and so on. The very fact that we find ourselves in a stress spiral or not feeling as fulfilled in life as we might be is an indication that there is more we need to learn. This is why many discoveries we make over the weeks may seem to be quite paradoxical. Many of our long-held assumptions may well be untrue. If they are untrue they will naturally lead to stress, dissatisfaction and disappointment rather than the anticipated happiness. It is useful for us to shed light on these assumptions and beliefs and, without throwing them out indiscriminately, we would do well to examine and test them. What stands the test stays, and what doesn't we can happily let go of as we move forward.

Model for the stress management program

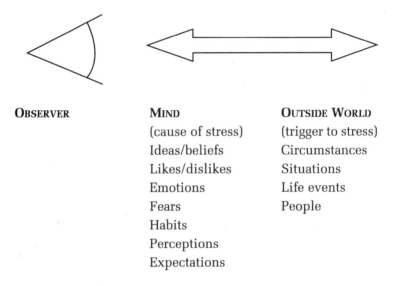

OBSERVER	MIND	OUTSIDE WORLD
	(cause of stress)	(trigger to stress)
	Ideas/beliefs	Circumstances
	Likes/dislikes	Situations
	Emotions	Life events
	Fears	People
	Habits	
	Perceptions	
	Expectations	

The above figure may help us to appreciate some core principles about the SRP. It illustrates the analogy of a rope under tension pulling us, or at least our peace of mind, off balance. We often find it hard to maintain our sense of equanimity in such conditions and our self-control is marked by tensions pulling against counter tensions as these ideas and emotions pull against each other and we struggle with events. Pulling one end of the rope is the outside world, full of people and events. The other end is held by what goes on in the mind in relation to these people and events. We can't necessarily control the outside world, but we do have some say about our attitude towards it. We may find that the cause of much of our stress is not the things that we usually blame. If we believe that our stress is only caused by what is going on around us then the assumption follows that in order to relieve our pain we have to control the people and events around us so as to 'get the world just the way I want it.' Well, good luck. Controlling the universe is a big job! Of course others, labouring under the same assumptions as us, are trying to do the same thing. This is not a recipe for stress-free living. It is a recipe for manipulation, failure, conflict and frustration.

> **'Man is buffeted by circumstances so long as he believes himself to be the creature of outside conditions, but when he realises that his is a creative power, and that he may command the hidden soil and seeds of his being out of which circumstances grow, then he becomes the rightful master of himself.'**
> —*James Allen,* As a Man Thinketh

What we come to find is that these outside events are simply the triggers. Sometimes they are also called 'stressors'. If we look carefully we may notice that what goes on in the mind is the cause of much of our tension and unease, but with care and attention we can have considerable control over it—not through the suppression of tension, but through its release—and in the process be able to work more in harmony with people and events.

Stress and perception

Let us expand a little more on this relationship between stress and the stressor. This will be the first of the eight tasks, but some preliminary remarks need to be made. If we stop and reflect for just a moment we become aware that we can sometimes experience considerable stress because of minor stressors. Furthermore, different people have different responses to the same events and situations depending on what they think about them. Some responses are more appropriate than others. Hence, an interesting challenge for one person may be a major stressor for another.

Consider a simple analogy. If two people see a rope one person might, due to inadequate light, mistakenly think it was a snake and so suffer enormous but unjustified stress, anxiety or fear. It may not be apparent to us at the moment, but most of the things over which we experience stress are actually ropes, not snakes. Another person, if they had a torch, might perceive the rope for what it is and put it to good use. The difference between stress and opportunity is generally no more than this.

Even something so unwanted as illness can be responded to differently. Many will see it as completely negative, but some find that it can be an opportunity to grow and learn about oneself. We can see that the thoughts and prejudices that we hold about events in our lives are cause of the response, not the events themselves. Each is in the same situation but each has *perceived* it differently. The best state of perception is to see clearly and broadly, but all too often we see things a little foggily or narrowly.

'We see through a glass darkly.'
—*Plato*
—Bible, Corinthians

'We do not see things as they are. We see things as we are.'
—*Talmud*

Sometimes when we make judgements about things we only have a limited or partial perception of the situation. Thus we can be quick to condemn a person when we have not seen the whole of their life in context, where they have come from, what they have had to experience and so on. We can easily get angry at a car driving too fast, but not see the woman in the back seat about to give birth. We can easily get angry at someone being late for an appointment, but not see the fact that they had a flat tyre. It does not mean that there is never be a time to get angry, but we can find, if we take care to look, that most of our stress and anger is based on a very limited and biased perception. We can be rash judges making pronouncements on poor quality evidence.

It cuts the other way also. We can be in the presence of a snake, but because of inadequate light assume that it is a rope and so unwittingly blunder into dangerous situations. Examples of this in life are many and varied, including being induced into taking drugs, being conned by someone into a business deal based on unrealistic promises, making ill-advised business decisions or making poor lifestyle and health decisions. In such cases there is inadequate awareness and weighing up of the situation. Oftentimes we look back and wonder what was in our heads when the poor decision was made. To avoid such dangers one needs to be awake and exercise reasonable caution. Fear and anxiety do not do the job. Awareness and reason do.

Furthermore, we frequently experience considerable stress due to the way we think when there is no stressor present at all. Mark Twain obviously recognised this when he said, 'I've had a lot of catastrophes in my life, and some of them actually happened.'

It is like we are responding to the imagination as if it were real. Consider how many times we have experienced anxiety when thinking about exams or anticipating public speaking long before the actual event. When the event finally comes around, the anxiety often disables us to a greater or lesser extent, or the event was nowhere near as bad as we made it out to be.

We can also re-experience stress time and again by going over past events such as arguments or mistakes. In reality the event is in the past and our mental replays are only mental projections, but we can so easily take them to be real. Noticing mental, emotional and physical reactions to such thoughts will indicate that, at least to some extent, we are taking the mental projection to be real. The stress will soon dissipate if we at least see the projection for what it is. It is like the experience of feeling a release of fear at a horror movie when we remember that we are just watching a movie.

What determines our reactions to people and events often has far less to do with the actual people or events than it has to do with all sorts of thoughts and feelings we have about them. Many of these are quite habitual, mechanical, imaginary or unreasonable and we hardly ever stop to examine their reasonableness or validity, let alone consider discarding them. When we see that we can stand back from thoughts and feelings and let go of the ones that are of little use, then we begin to develop self-determination, purposeful action and freedom in our lives. This, in a manner of speaking, is where real self-control or autonomy begins.

Observing different states of the mind

To recap on the preceding discussion, it is not just the presence of stress-provoking thoughts that causes our stress, but the relationship we bring to them.

There are all sorts of things that go through our minds which constantly colour our responses to, and ability to deal with, daily life. The first thing in stress management—in fact its cornerstone—is to shed a bit of light (awareness) upon what is going through the mind so as to be able to see which ideas and motives are worth retaining and which are irrational, distorting, unrealistic and obstructive. Becoming aware of thoughts, motives and feelings and letting go of the harmful ones is where stress management and effective action begin. Freedom, without awareness, is not a viable option.

> 'Eternal vigilance is the price of liberty.'
> —John Curran

For much of the day our minds are concerned not just with thoughts that are relevant and useful, but with all sorts of superfluous and often irrational mental activity such as fears, apprehensions and regrets. Sometimes we call it day-dreaming, and like dreaming in the night, it can be nightmarish and full of anxiety. As has already been mentioned, this day-dreaming can take the form of replaying past events and imagining future events, having conversations with ourselves, worrying or thinking about being somewhere else. It is as if life is going on in the here and now, but for much of the day we are 'absent minded'—that is, our thoughts are somewhere else. Much more of this absent mindedness goes on than we are aware of, but just as the relief from a nightmare comes when we awaken, so too can we resolve much of our stress by finding ways to reduce, or wake up from, this superfluous activity in the mind. If we are unaware of its presence we cannot do anything about it.

Superfluous mental activity prevents us from making clear contact with people and events around us. When this happens we are far less able to respond appropriately. The more active the mind gets the greater the disconnection gets; the more clear and focused the mind the more connected, effective and unburdened we become. This mental activity is often most obvious to us when we try to stop and be quiet, like when we go to bed or try to practise these relaxation techniques we have heard so much about. The mindfulness exercise is the single most important practice, helping to re-establish this connection and let go of distractions so as to unburden the mind. The release of this mental activity clears the mind and eases stress, and the greater attentiveness this brings can assist in efficiency and competence.

> 'If water derives lucidity from stillness, how much more the faculties of the mind! The mind of the sage, being in repose, becomes the mirror of the universe.'
> —*Chuang Tzu*

31

What effect does this mental activity have?

In a distracted state of mind our responses and behaviour can be very automatic, habitual and inappropriate to the present situation. We can see the evidence for and result of this sort of mental activity. The way it makes us lose contact is obvious in commonplace examples such as:

- Noticing ourselves studying a textbook and taking nothing in because we are so preoccupied about what might be on the exam or how well are we going to do; hence study becomes laborious and time-consuming.
- Holding a conversation and not hearing what someone says, perhaps because we are still going over a previous conversation or anticipating a later one; hence all sorts of mistakes, misunderstandings and misinterpretations arise.
- Having an argument with someone in our own minds even before we have seen them; hence this prejudiced the discussion even before it has taken place.
- Driving a car and not remembering a thing about the trip—we might be thinking of what we are going to do when we arrive at our destination, or what we were previously doing; hence the risk of car accidents arises through not paying attention to the road.
- Someone introduces themselves and we immediately forget their name because we are so concerned about the impression we might make.
- Waiting for the weather report only to find that our attention went off just at the moment that tomorrow's temperature was being read out.

We have probably noticed that in such a state of disconnection, working efficiently becomes harder, communication tends to be disjointed and incomplete, a lot of time is wasted, we assert ourselves inappropriately, mistakes are made, solutions to problems take a lot longer to find, learning is difficult and memory is inefficient. Hamlet had the problem of having a clouded mind and so did not know what to do:

'**And thus the native hue of resolution**
is sicklied o'er with the pale cast of thought,
and enterprises of great pitch and moment.
With this regard their currents turn awry,
and lose the name of action.'
—Hamlet iii.1

It is no coincidence that Shakespeare begins this speech with, 'To be or not to be, that is the question.' He seems to be exhorting Hamlet to meditate a little and clear his mind before acting. When the mind is alert and clear, efficiency improves, we understand people better, we make ourselves better understood, time is managed better, we assert ourselves more reasonably, fewer mistakes are made, solutions are more easily discovered, learning is more efficient and memory is more acute. Amid this fog of disconnected mental activity resides most of our stress and inability to deal effectively with everyday life.

We need to clear this 'pale cast of thought' so that we can see and respond better and in the process find the ability to be in increasingly difficult and trying situations and still feel at peace with ourselves. Effective stress management is certainly not about avoiding what we find difficult but more about learning to meet it in a different way.

Where am I among all this?

Let us return to the model mentioned previously. It is important to distinguish between the observer of the stress, the stress and the stressor. We might consider ourselves the observer or the subject, standing back from it all and just watching what goes on around us—the object. This is what it means to be objective. In times of considerable stress and anxiety, to use an analogy, it is like being in the middle of a hurricane—it is important to remember that there is still the peaceful and quiet eye of the hurricane, or a safe sanctuary, while everything blows around us. T S Elliot described this as 'The still point of the turning world.'

The first step is to cultivate this ability to just watch what goes on without any particular desire to get involved or change anything. Often standing back and observing in a detached way is enough to ease the pressure of the situation. It is as though these fearful and anxiety producing ideas start to buffet us less and less. In this respect the relaxation exercise is all-important in fostering the ability to observe and let go. This is not denial or cutting off. It is simply that learning to be more objective can help us to respond more consciously.

When the tensions and all the energy they consume are released then the mind, in a clearer state, is more able to weigh things up. Put another way, we can be more reasonable, see things in perspective and make more balanced choices. From the point of the attentive observer we can let the mind function more effectively and naturally.

What does it mean to let go? Is this another way of copping out? Not if it is done reasonably. Let us come back to the rope analogy and its two ends being placed under tension. As we will see later, it is possible to mentally let go of tension. This needs to be done, not in a careless way, but rather in a constructive, careful and gentle way by practising letting go of what is false, silly, destructive or unreasonable. Letting go does not mean turning away from situations that present themselves. It means responding attentively but without the impediment of tension.

Paradox 4: Being less concerned about the result helps to remove the pressure and so makes it easier to work with the process effectively.

The more rigid and fixed our thinking becomes, the more 'ropes' there are that can potentially pull us off balance. Life becomes a constant struggle in an apparently threatening environment. The tensions within the mind are the things that tend to pull us apart and set us at odds with ourselves.

People who practise this sort of approach soon find a new sort of self-control. In essence it is like shift from a state where we are controlled by habitual and unhelpful thoughts, desires, fears and emotions, to one where we are our own person again, able to use reason and make choices. Furthermore, in this state it is a lot easier to lead a more balanced lifestyle.

What about happiness?

Happiness is an elusive state to which we all aspire and yet it does not take too long observing a child to realise that we were born with a simple and innocent form of happiness. Where did it go? What covered it up such that we almost forgot we ever had it? In a search to reclaim it we act out our lives and can be observed to do the strangest and most contradictory things as a result. We pursue what we assume will make us happy and try often desperately to avoid what we think will make us unhappy.

What we come to realise in moments when we stop and 'just be' is that we feel better quite naturally. We did not have to do or get anything. It just happens when we allow it but we are hardly ever unconcerned enough with the preoccupations of the mind to let it happen. There is an old story about a man who searched high and low for his glasses but could not find them anywhere. He nearly gave up in total dejection until he realised that he could not find them because they were sitting on his forehead. Meditation and the peace that sometimes comes with it, if we should be so lucky, teaches us that what we look for may be very close to us, so close in fact that we already have it.

> **Paradox 5: As much as we aspire to happiness we hardly ever allow ourselves to experience it.**
>
> **Paradox 6: Our search for happiness is a search for something we already have.**

Is self-criticism of any use?

The process of mindfulness, as has been mentioned, will make us more aware of our thoughts and motives and we will also find that some of them are not so pleasant to look at. If we wish to make progress as we proceed though the SRP it is of vital importance that criticism of oneself or others is not entertained. It is one thing to objectively see mistakes and correct them; it is another to put ourselves down because of them. The former is helpful and constructive and the latter is unhelpful and destructive. It literally sabotages self-growth. A good policy is to never speak of ourselves or others with any sort of destructive or harmful intent. This includes thoughts spoken in the mind. Once we notice our attention going back to such thoughts, we should practise letting them go. The consistent awareness that they tend to harm ourselves and lead nowhere useful will help to increase our motivation. We soon discover that one of the signs of a greater understanding of ourselves is a greater tolerance and compassion for ourselves and others.

Meditation and eliciting the relaxation response

The human body has an immense capacity to heal itself given the right conditions. Unfortunately stress and other factors can interfere with this healing taking place naturally. In order to facilitate healing, therefore, one needs to remove the impediments. It is also true of the mind. It will naturally move towards happiness, peace and equanimity if it is given the right conditions. This can be done effectively through the relaxation response. This term refers to a coordinated and calm state of mind and body that is associated with peak efficiency and effectiveness.

The relaxation response can be elicited in a number of ways. Many of these techniques can be used on their own or in combination with others.

- Soothing and harmonious music is commonly used. Some forms of music can, however, increase stress and negative states of mind. This seems to be independent of personal preference.
- Regular moderate physical exercise is often used by people to relax, but excessive exercise can be a stress on mind and body.
- Gaining wider popularity in Western culture are long-tried techniques from the East like Tai Chi and Yoga. They incorporate physical movement but importantly make great efforts to cultivate a mindful state in the process. There are other techniques that cultivate awareness through movement, such as the Feldenkrais and Alexander techniques.
- In more recent times other techniques are used such as hypnosis and biofeedback which need specialised training and/or equipment.
- There are also significant benefits that many experience through spiritual disciplines like prayer and confession.
- Creative pursuits, arts and self-expression can all be very useful.
- Good communication skills and effective time management are often learned for more pragmatic reasons, but they can have the side-effect of helping people to be more relaxed.

The most conscious, researched and focused ways, however, of specifically inducing the relaxation response are through the variety of meditative and relaxation exercises. Every culture has had its contemplative and meditative practices for this purpose. Whichever way we choose among all these ways will need to be in an appropriate form for us personally and culturally. None of these ways, meditation included, requires us to join a monastery, take on an ideology nor to give up our roles in life. Any process will need to work in with our life as a whole.

Meditation is about more than just relaxing the body, as useful as that is. It is about the mind. What is meditation? There is no one answer to this, but perhaps one way of expressing it is to call it a simple 'way of being'.

Meditative exercises can be practised for many reasons, from the most mundane to the most profound. We might take up meditation to help reduce our blood pressure or to increase resistance to disease by reversing the immune-suppressing effects of stress. We might wish to learn to cope better with life's stresses or improve productivity. We might wish to overcome performance anxiety. We might wish to understand ourselves better. We might see meditation as a spiritual and contemplative practice. We might also find that our reasons for learning to meditate mature or deepen over time so that what was originally of central importance gradually becomes of peripheral importance and what was of peripheral importance soon becomes of central importance. The point is however, that it must be practical for us and relevant to our needs. That said, whatever reason we practise it for, all the beneficial side-effects tend to come with it.

Mindfulness has a long tradition in east and west but in modern times it has gone through something of a renaissance and is increasingly the source of scientific investigation. Meditation exercises all involve some form of concentration, but not the usual state we think of as concentration of intensity or pressure. Rather, they teach the mind how to *rest*. For it to rest and focus it has to learn to *let go* of all the distractions. Thus focus and relaxation naturally go together.

Paradox 7: We cannot and need not *make* the mind still—trying to still the mind by force has the opposite effect. We can experience stillness by not being moved by the movements of the mind and senses.

Regular practise of these exercises are the cornerstone of the practical part of this program. The term 'relaxation exercise' is sometimes used, but it should be noted that this is an exercise in waking up and being more aware. Through this waking up and the cultivation of restful alertness, one may feel more relaxed and free of psychological and therefore physical tension, but relaxation in the sense we mean it here is not about going to sleep or off into a dream; quite the opposite. The overactive or burdened mind also makes it more difficult to sleep and so these exercises may, if practised regularly, also lead to better and healthier sleep patterns.

Relaxation and meditation exercises are not the answer to all of life's problems. We cannot open our eyes and make everything we don't like in the world go away. What we can do is help some of our negative thoughts and emotions to clear, which certainly makes it easier to deal with what we need to and also makes it obvious that many things we saw as problems were not really problems at all. As such, meditation can be a cornerstone of a total approach which may include counselling, CBT, problem-solving or mindfulness-based stress management. Such exercises are like a training ground for the mind that can facilitate these other processes. The awareness that is fostered through meditation, for example, can help enormously with cognitive approaches that are aimed at sorting through irrational and distracting thoughts.[41]

> 'Concentration is the secret of strength . . . in all the
> management of human affairs.'
> —*Ralph Waldo Emerson*

The practice one undertakes on a twice-daily basis is not just meant as a nice time-out in an awful day, but rather as something which better prepares body and mind to be able to meet the demands of the day.

Meditation as a contemplative practice has many interpretations and varieties and there are many misunderstandings about them. In essence it relies on a combination of concentration and relaxation, attentiveness and calmness. Most techniques will rely on the attention being focussed or rested on a focal point. In the process one learns *not to struggle* with unnecessary and distracting mental activity, which is so often full of anxieties, fears, negativity and criticism. One quickly learns in experience that this reactivity feeds and strengthens the distractions and anxieties. Instead one cultivates the ability to be aware of them but to be *less reactive* to them. One learns to let go of them and they soon go of their own accord.

> 'When forced, as it seems, by thine environment to be utterly
> disquieted, return with all speed into thyself, staying in
> discord no longer than thou must. By constant recurrence to
> the harmony thou wilt gain more command over it.'
> —*Marcus Aurelius*

To use an analogy, our thoughts are often like angry barking dogs that do not give us much peace. The quickest way to be free of them is to be unmoved by them. Fighting or running only leads them to bite us or chase us. What one practises is not denial or suppression. What one learns is a simple freedom that comes from finally understanding that we can choose to take up—or not take up—thoughts and emotions.

To use another analogy, like being in a market, we can choose to buy what we wish but we need to learn to take the better and leave the worse. In this analogy the capital or cash that we spend—be it wisely or unwisely—is our attention.

In a manner of speaking, we are all meditating on something or other nearly all of the time. What one gives one's attention to is what we meditate upon, for better or for worse. In due course this is what we become. As the saying goes, 'as a man (or woman) thinketh, so he (or she) becomes.' This simple principle is at the heart of many self-help programs and affirmations aimed at helping people to be successful. If one feeds a lot of angry thoughts then one is practising anger and one can soon becomes 'expert' at it. It is the same with kind or compassionate thoughts. Unfortunately, this process of meditating on negative and unhelpful thoughts is going on all the time unconsciously and we have largely lost the ability to stop even when we choose. We may not think that we practise mantra meditation, for example, but if we have a thought which we habitually churn in our mind then, in a manner of speaking, that is our mantra. Our mantras may not be altogether useful. We might habitually repeat to ourselves ideas like 'I can't cope,' or 'I'm not loveable,' or 'I'm hopeless.' These are not particularly useful 'mantras'. It is far better to consciously focus our attention on something more truthful or productive. It is in this way that people often use mantra meditation, prayer or affirmations.

Varieties of meditation exercises

The following table lists some meditative practices which can be used to remedy this problem. People classify these practices in varying ways so the following is only one way of looking at them.

Varieties of meditation and relaxation exercises

Physical relaxation.

1. Progressive Muscle Relaxation (PMR): Physical muscle tension is a direct result of a mental tension or 'holding on'. It is aimed at relaxation of the body only which, though useful, is but the first step in meditation. There are other varieties also including the deep physical relaxation of Yoga Nidra.

Exercises utilising thought.

2. Visualisation, affirmations and imagery: These practices can help to settle a distracted or anxious mind to some extent and also encourage attitude change. They can help to displace negative conditioned thoughts by conditioning more positive thoughts. They are also sometimes used to tap into unconscious thought patterns and memories and bring them to the surface; hence they can sometimes overlap with the use of music and art therapies.

Exercises aimed at transcending thought.

3. Mindfulness: This includes concentration on the *breath*, which is found in many mindfulness and some yoga exercises or focussing on one or all of the *five senses*, for example listening. The mental clarity and focus often produced is echoed in phrases such as 'coming to our senses' or 'getting in touch'. Such exercises bring the mind into a state of greater perceptiveness in the present moment.

4. Mantra meditation: This has been practised in most cultures throughout history.* The mantra, as the focus of attention, is a word or phrase repeated silently in the mind and is given preference to the usual mental

---

* Transcendental Meditation (TM) and the ancient form of Benedictine meditation as revived by the Christian Meditation Network both use mantra meditation, as do many other groups.

agitation and distraction so that it is gently allowed to settle.

5. Prayer: Many people use prayer as a meditative or contemplative practice. There are many similarities between prayer and mantra meditation although in prayer the words repeated will have obvious spiritual meaning to the person praying. In the process there is the aim of transcending distracted or mundane thought in order to become absorbed in contemplation on a 'higher' plane of thought. In a manner of speaking, both mantra meditation and prayer use a thought in order to transcend thought.

Many people's first experiences with meditation will be through visualisation. This is quite a different approach to mindfulness. One of the problems with the mind's tendency to visualise and imagine is that it is actually the source of much of our stress and maladaptive coping strategies (as discussed earlier). We spend most of our day unconsciously and habitually visualising. It takes many forms including 'catastrophising', 'awfulising' and pre-judging events. Having progressively lost the ability to distinguish between reality and imagination, we unfortunately get lost in our thoughts. This form of unconscious and habitual mental activity is of a different nature to the conscious use of creative imagination that is used by many artists, composers and inventors. Mindfulness can help us to see the unhelpful tendency of the mind to visualise for what it is and also help us to more consciously tap into the intuitive creative abilities of the mind.

Different forms of meditation suit different people, but whichever form is chosen they all need practise and perseverance in order to be effective. There is little use in thinking in terms of success, criticism or failure—you should just practise. Having said that, higher commitment and a sincere and respectful attitude will naturally speed any progress. With experience comes learning how to meditate more deeply. Anxiety about results or progress impedes the process. Meditation should be kept simple and easy. If it is becoming difficult or complicated then one should seek guidance. There is an old saying that one should practise with a 'beginner's mind'—there is much wisdom in that. Too much thinking and theorising about the process will not be useful.

The clinical uses of meditation

Meditative techniques are increasingly being used in clinical practice for both groups and individuals.[36] Fortunately, benefits can be just as marked for the therapist as they are for the patients.

Of the various forms of meditation the most researched and used in the contemporary scientific and therapeutic contexts are mindfulness meditation and mantra meditation, of which TM is the most widely used and researched form. As a stress reduction technique mindfulness meditation and mindfulness-based stress management has also been clearly shown to be powerfully therapeutic—for the medical profession and medical students as well.[37,38] Advantages demonstrated in these studies include reduced anxiety, distress and depression, and increased empathy, self-control and spiritual experiences.

One of the most attractive aspects of this simple form of therapy is that the side-effects, be they physical or psychological, seem to be so beneficial. When coming to such practices ourselves or in introducing them to others it is important to deal with the person's relevant agenda—whether it is learning to relieve anxiety[39] or to help prevent relapse in depression.[40,41] Meditation can be a useful adjunct in the treatment of many diverse clinical situations such as coping with cancer[42], fibromyalgia[43] and chronic pain,[44] learning to study better, using it as an adjunct to the management of eating disorders,[45] hypertension,[46] cardiovascular disease[47] or asthma.[48] It is sometimes used as therapy on its own, or sometimes as part of a holistic approach including lifestyle change, such as in the Ornish program for reversing heart disease.[49] There is still an enormous need for further research to test the application, efficacy and safety of practices like mindfulness more fully, but one would have to say on the basis of the presently available evidence that the prospects look extremely encouraging.

There are few contraindications for meditation, but states of acute psychosis would probably be one. In such states there may for the time being be little insight and objectivity about what is in the mind. That having been said, if there is some insight then the person can learn to gently deflect their attention away from hallucinations or delusional thoughts. There is little evidence presently about the use of meditation for psychosis in remission and so one should exercise caution if it is to be used in such cases and it should not be used to replace the appropriate use of necessary medication. It may be more appropriate to engage the person mindfully in very tactile and practical activities and hobbies. Careful supervision should be exercised if it is used. Although meditation can help with severe depression it is generally better to use it in conjunction with other therapies as required. In time the meditation may help to get closer to the thoughts that cause and aggravate depression in a much deeper way than the medication can.

Meditation, like physical exercise, is not always easy, but this does not mean that it is not being helpful. This is not a contraindication to practising it or a sign that the meditation is not doing its work, but it does sound a note of care. Occasionally a person can find that, like turning on a light, the greater awareness generated by meditation can initially make certain thoughts, memories and fears that may be lying just below conscious awareness more obvious and disturbing. Some of these thoughts can be quite strong—one needs some courage and patience. It is best to proceed gently and never to force oneself or someone else to proceed unwillingly if such worrying thoughts arise. It is important to remind ourselves to see the thoughts as they are: images and feelings based on past experience rising and falling on the surface of their awareness. In this way a person learns self-control by staying with the awareness rather than being reactive to what they are aware of, much like learning to watch the movie while remembering that it is just a movie. With patience one learns to have considerable control over such thoughts and mental images by detaching from them, and they can soon lose their emotive power. From there it is easier to re-engage with the issues we need to deal with, decisions we need to make, discussions we need to have.

Meditation as a spiritual practice

For many the ultimate aim of meditative and contemplative practices is the spiritual, philosophical and self-knowledge aspects, but a person always proceeds at their own pace and in their own way. One may find over time that what was originally of central importance, such as the clinical and practical uses of meditation, becomes of more peripheral importance, and what was originally of peripheral importance, such as the spiritual aspects, becomes more central, but at every stage the process should be relevant to the person's needs. It should be offered and never imposed on someone and it needs to be in a form appropriate to the person's culture and beliefs.

As meditation matures over time it leads to a deeper sense of peace, unity and consciousness and so it is not difficult to see that meditation and spirituality can complement each other quite naturally. Prayer, of course, is in many ways a very particular and focused form of spiritual meditation.

'Meditation . . . breaks down all the barriers set up within us, between our outer and inner life and brings the whole of us into harmony. The peace of Christ, which is beyond all understanding, beyond all analysis, arises from this unity.'
—*Fr John Main,* Moment of Christ

When the mind, completely controlled, is centred in the Self,
and free from all earthly desires, then is the man truly
spiritual. . . . There, where the whole nature is seen in the light
of the Self, where the man abides within his Self and is
satisfied, there, its functions restrained by its union with the
divine, the mind finds rest.
—*Bhagavad Gita*

The mindfulness exercises

'Be strong, and enter into your own body: for there your
foothold is firm. Consider it well, O my heart! Go not
elsewhere! Put all imaginations away, and stand fast in that
which you are.'
—*Kabir*

We use the term 'mindfulness exercise'. It can, in some ways,
also be called a relaxation exercise, but it should be noted that
this is an exercise in waking up and being more aware. There can
be a lot of misconceptions about what meditation is but one way
of looking at mindfulness is that it is little more that learning to
tune the mind in, not tune out. There are different forms of these
exercises. Outlined below is one exercise that has particular
relevance to the SRP and the eight practical tasks that follow.
The SRP has been run for medical, professional and lay
audiences since 1991. The principles and practices are contemporary and yet very old at the same time.

Preparation

It is often easier to practise the exercise in a quiet place without
interruptions, but this is not always possible. Noise need not
preclude the practice at all; but we may notice that in a stimu-
lating environment the activity of the mind is increased greatly,

so we just have to practise bringing the attention back more frequently than would otherwise be the case.

It is recommended that the exercise be practised for at least five minutes twice daily (before breakfast and dinner are good times) and at other times during the day if needed. These other times could take only a minute, or even a few seconds, just to help break the build-up of tension throughout the day. Before food is preferable—after food one can too easily become sleepy.

Over time, according to your level of motivation, you can build up the time to 10, 15 or even 20 minutes twice a day. If you are practising another form of relaxation exercise or meditation it is not necessarily recommended that you stop doing it, especially if you have found it helpful; however, this exercise is specifically adapted to the SRP so to get the most out of the SRP it is important to practise the mindfulness exercise regularly. Speed of progress will naturally be enhanced by regularity and commitment.

While practising this exercise, there is no need to 'try' or put in effort, except in so far as we remember to bring the attention back when it wanders off. Don't be perturbed if mental activity continues throughout; that does not necessarily mean that we are doing something wrong or that the exercise is not beneficial. The important thing is to practise letting go, or not feeding the unwanted activity with attention, because it is attention that gives this distracted thinking its power. Practise allowing each phase of the exercise to occur effortlessly. Trying excessively to make an experience happen will increase tension and mental activity.

Position

Sit in an *upright, balanced but relaxed position* with the back and neck straight and held without unnecessary tension, and with the hands resting on the lap. A 'lazy' posture that is too comfortable will become an exercise in going to sleep, not waking up; if the body is uncomfortable or unbalanced this too will have a distracting effect on the mind. Some choose to practise the exercise lying down. This can also be satisfactory if the back is straight and the body symmetrically positioned. Many people find this position too readily leads to sleep, which might be useful in the middle of the night but is not generally useful during the day. A power nap can be good if one has the opportunity, but it is not meditation.

Once you have found the posture let the eyes gently close and begin the exercise. The practice is very simple; in short it is a matter of resting the attention with something and being uninterested in everything else. This does not mean that one has to block everything else out. In this form it will have three phases:

- PMR
- Breathing
- Listening

A mindfulness meditation

Become aware of your presence in the room, here and now, and just rest in that, letting thoughts of past and future pass.

Progressive Muscle Relaxation

Be conscious of the body and let it fall still. Now, become aware of each part of the body and release muscle tension patiently, consciously and methodically. Start with the feet and then move to the legs, stomach, back, hands, arms, shoulders, neck and face. There is no rush. If one becomes aware of any tension coming back into the body just practise letting it go again. The important thing to remember is that one does not have to make oneself relax, it is more a matter of 'allowing'. Having spent some time going through each part of the body, help the relaxation to deepen by taking a few deep breaths and slowly letting them out, and with the out-breath let any extra muscle tension fall away. Let the body feel its full weight. Then let the breathing fall into its own natural rhythm, gentle and smooth, without interference.

Breathing

Observe and **feel** the breath. Rest the attention where the air enters and leaves the body, whether that be through the nose or the mouth. Maintain this for a few minutes. During this or any other stage of the exercise distracting thoughts and feelings may come into the mind, like images on a movie screen, or a train of thought tending to carry the attention away with it. There is no need to try and stop these thoughts coming into mind, because this will just serve to make them worse. Let them be observed and let them pass again, allowing the attention to return gently but without hesitation to an awareness of the breath. We are not able to necessarily stop the thoughts and day-dreams, but we can practise standing back, observing, detaching and letting go of them. This includes happy day-dreams as well as unhappy ones. We are practising waking up out of day-dreams and becoming aware in the present; that is presence of mind, not absent-mindedness.

Listening

For a few minutes just listen to all the sounds you can hear around you. Let them come and go. Listen as far out to the horizon as you can. There is no need to think about the sounds, what they mean or anything else. Just listen and rest, once again letting thoughts and feelings pass as they arise. Choose once again to gently direct the listening from any chatter or noise in the mind and to reconnect it with the physical sounds.

At the completion of this phase take a deep breath in and out, gently open the eyes, and when ready, mindfully move into the activities which await you. Mindfulness does not end at the end of this practice. It teaches us a conscious way of living: a way of living mindfully.

Many people say that they 'fail' this exercise, that they are not able to stop the thoughts or let go of all the tensions. There is no need to stop them, nor is there a need to engage in them. There is no such thing as failing the exercise. It is more a matter of observing whatever is going on. The idea of success and failure just feeds more of the thinking going on in the mind—thinking that needs to be let go of. The important thing is just to practise it. If the mind remains active don't worry, just practise not getting caught up with the activity. While noting it, and the sorts of things which tend to repeat, just learn to be objective about it. In a manner of speaking, learn to be less moved by it. This takes a lot of the force out of these thoughts and therefore gives us a significant level of freedom from them.

Paradox 8: What we practise we get good at, whether it be getting stressed or finding peace of mind. Unfortunately we often practise things that are unhelpful and avoid practising things that are helpful.

The eight mindfulness tasks

Task 1:	**Perception**
Task 2:	**Letting go and acceptance**
Task 3:	**Presence of mind**
Task 4:	**Limitations**
Task 5:	**Listening**
Task 6:	**Self-discipline**
Task 7:	**Emotions**
Task 8:	**Expanding self-interest**

These mindfulness tasks are a practical way to extend our awareness and stress-coping strategies into more and more of the day. They extend the skills we practise in the mindfulness exercise and apply them to practical situations. They are not designed to be accepted on face value, but rather to be explored, questioned and investigated.

The tasks help us to reflect upon some of the thought processes behind our stress and to explore alternate ways of thinking and seeing which might help us to relieve stress. It would be useful to take on one of these tasks each week and practise it. If this book is being read as a companion to doing the SRP in a group then this task will be debriefed in the following week at which time you will be asked about your:

- Observations
- Experiences
- Insights
- Questions

In the group discussion you should only offer what you feel comfortable discussing with the group. It might also be useful to record your weekly observations, experiences, insights and questions in a journal.

Task 1: Perception

Do we ever make mountains out of molehills? Do we ever get things out of perspective without even knowing it? Do we ever come to judgements without seeing the whole picture? Do we ever make problems for ourselves that don't even exist? If we do any of these sorts of things, as we all do, we might have a little to learn about perception and stress. Let us revisit the story about the man and the snake.

A man is walking down a bush track at dusk. On the track about five metres ahead he sees something. It is black, about two metres long, and is coiled up. 'It's a snake'. He starts shaking in fear that the snake will sense his presence and make a lunge at him. Furthermore, there are probably other snakes in the vicinity. Paralysed with fear, he can't move. Luckily, coming along behind him is the park ranger, who has a torch and he asks why the man is so anxious. The man tells the ranger about the snake. The ranger says, 'Well we had better investigate,' so he shines the torch on the 'snake'. Shedding a little more light on the object it is immediately apparent that the snake is merely a rope. The snake never actually existed, except in the fertile imagination of the man. His anxiety was based on what he mistakenly perceived was there but which did not actually exist outside of his own imagination.

Under certain circumstances a fight or flight response can be quite appropriate and healthy, for example, when we are in the presence of an actual poisonous snake. Often we think that the world is full of snakes that aren't there, however, and the world appears to be a far more threatening place than it is. The important tools we have are the torch (awareness) and the power to investigate (reason). It is reasonable to investigate things. If we are not aware we will not see the snakes that are there until it is too late, but we need to be careful about the conclusions we

jump to. Even if it is a snake, panic or high stress will not be the
most useful response but evasive action or even snake charming
(which is little more than learning to master our fears and cope
with stressful situations competently) might be. People who
learn to deal clearly and decisively with adversity find that there
is less and less to fear about it. Healthy caution, born of clear
perception, is different to unhealthy stress or fear and is a part of
coping well.

Our perceptiveness, awareness and richness of experience
tends to dim over time as we grow up. Impressions are very full
and rich for children—that is why they find the world such as
fascinating place.

> 'Shades of the prison-house begin to close
> Upon the growing boy.
> But he beholds the light, and whence it flows,
> He sees it in his joy;
> The youth, who daily farther from the east
> Must travel, still is Nature's priest,
> And by the vision splendid
> Is on his way attended.
> At length the man perceives it die away
> And fade into the light of common day.'
> —*Henry Wordsworth,* Recollections of Early Childhood

Just as we can have an object in our physical eye which affects
our ability to see clearly, so too can these thoughts, assumptions,
expectations, pre-judgements, opinions, habits and feelings be
like impediments in our mind's eye. So it is that when two
people are in exactly the same situation they can have entirely
different perceptions of the event. Similarly, the same person can
have entirely different reactions to the same event at different
times depending on their state of mind. For example, if we are at
ease with ourselves then we will be far less likely to make a big
deal out of a rude or off-handed comment by a friend. We may

even be able to notice that the comment might be coming from some anxiety or misunderstanding on their part. If, for example, our awareness and self-esteem are very low then the same comment can seem like the end of the world.

If one perceives events clearly and on their merits then the response can be appropriate to the situation, but if the view is obscured then the response, although well intentioned, will tend to be inappropriate because we are not responding to what is really there but to the idea we have projected. We can use negative emotions like stress, fear and anxiety as warning bells to awaken us to the possibility that we need to have another clearer look at the situation before us.

It is a strange thing, but ordinary people who do extraordinary things in crisis situations describe a state of high perceptiveness combined with calmness, fearlessness and responsiveness. Many would describe this as a transcendent experience, but if it is not understood such experiences can cause some confusion afterwards. The anxiety often comes in later when the mind fills with images of what might have happened.

Put another way, it is not the object that looks fearful or attractive; the fear or desirability arises from the thoughts we dress the object in. Removing these obscuring thoughts and feelings first requires that we see them, so the mindfulness exercise will help us in being aware of them and letting them go (or washing them out of the mind's eye). Eventually, as we come to perceive more clearly and thereby respond more effectively, we can come to be at ease in the most surprising situations and at the same time deal with them far more effectively. Effective stress management will not be well founded on ignoring what needs our attention. If we investigate for even a short time we appreciate that we need to cultivate a clearer perception of the world and its stressors in order to deal with them better. A more stress free perception doesn't mean creating an artificially rosy perception of the world, though. Having a pleasant day-dream while going through a red light in one's car will not lessen the pain or the expense.

If we cast our minds back we will remember that a stressor is defined as a situation, event, circumstance or person to which we attribute our experience of stress, but do they need to be stressors?

> **'After experience had taught me that the common occurrences of ordinary life are vain and futile, and I saw that all the objects of my desire and fear were in themselves nothing good or bad, save in so far as the mind was affected by them: I at length determined to search out whether there was not something truly good.'**
> —*Spinoza*

Consider the events that tend to trigger our stress. Consider the stressor and how we look at it in order to understand the origin of our stress better. When we see something, through the mind's eye as it were, do we see it on its own, just as it is? Or do we see it together with all sorts of habitual past thoughts, memories, opinions and feelings about it, some of which may be pleasant and others unpleasant, some well informed and others not so well informed? Does this make us less able to judge things on their actual merits and therefore less able to respond to them appropriately?

If those thoughts and feelings are very negative then we experience stress and avoidance. Consider further some simple examples of the relationship between perceptions and stress. People have all sorts of reactions to mice, and one would have to admit that many are totally out of proportion to the actual threat. When seeing a mouse, if one perceives a monster then one can experience an exaggerated stress response. This principle can be further illustrated with other commonplace examples. The dentist's surgery, for example, provides an excellent opportunity for studying stress management principles. A person with a toothache sees a dentist coming towards them and feels extremely fearful because of all the ideas and fears they have accumulated from the past about dentists, not because of any real or tangible discomfort in the present moment. When the pain comes, although it is generally not great, it causes a disproportionate amount of suffering because our perception of the pain is exaggerated by our anxieties or fears. It is not taken on its merits. A very good remedy is to see if the mouse really is a monster or whether the sensations while in the dentist's chair are really as terrible as we fear that they are. In other words, we can consciously and deliberately pay attention. It is exactly because we do not pay attention that we keep re-experiencing such stress and anxiety. The same sorts of reactions occur all day long to a greater or lesser extent in response to virtually every daily occurrence where stress arises.

Paradoxically, our pleasant habitual thoughts, expectations and mental projections can be just as distracting and troublesome as the unpleasant ones and also lead to inappropriate action. Consider the fact that the things we are most attracted to such as food, comfort, flattery or possessions often cause us the most trouble. With regard to the things we find pleasant it is easy to think that more is better and that they will provide a deeper and more lasting happiness than they actually can. This is also a distortion or mistake of perception. As such we can become dependent on things rather than perceiving the larger picture. Consider the influence that psychological addictions and dependencies can have on a person's life, which are only the earnest search for happiness in a place where it can't be found. Often, in reality, these things can lead to significant suffering in the longer term rather than the anticipated happiness. It is almost like trying to quench our thirst by drinking a mirage: just another distortion of perception.

There seems to be an important and intimate relationship between awareness, peacefulness and centeredness which can be summed up in the following quote from Milton: 'He that hath light may sit in the centre and enjoy bright day.'

Practice for the week: *Investigate the relationship between stress and perception in your own day-to-day life. In our minds are we creating stressors which don't exist? Are we getting things out of perspective by making mountains out of molehills? Are we ignoring issues which do need attention? If and when stress arises, don't regret it. Instead take the opportunity to take a fresh look at the so-called stressor.*

Task 2: Letting go and acceptance

'So free we seem so fettered we are.'
—*Robert Browning*

The first thing is to begin to hone our powers of observation, but now we need to practise letting go. During daily activity or at times when we are practising the mindfulness exercise we may notice that things float into the mind that we seem to latch onto—these are the source of our emotional and physical tension. A mental letting go is the first step in alleviating this situation. It is this that allows release from the physical tension that results from latching onto things. If we remember the rope analogy we can see that we try to maintain peace and equilibrium by mentally pulling against things all day. This creates tension within ourselves which often flows on to work-mates, parents, siblings, spouses and children. It often feels like the tug of war between ourselves and the world goes on all day.

It may seem so obvious that it hardly needs saying, but to feel relaxed we do not actually have to do anything. We merely have to *let go* of tension. Similarly, to feel untroubled by worry we simply need to let go of the thought causing it and get on with what we need to. If our house is burning down and the thought is 'call the fire brigade', then that is a useful thought to act upon. If a mistake has been made and the thought is rectifying it, then act on it. One type of thought is fruitless and stress-laden and the other useful and stress-relieving.

Our experience of mindfulness soon teaches us that when we are less preoccupied with the stress-provoking thoughts we feel happier and more peaceful. In a manner of speaking we become happier by *letting go* of unhappiness. In like manner, we come to understand things by *letting go* of misunderstandings we have about them. Notice that what arises in the mind doesn't have a hold on us; rather we have a hold on it. In a way it is like choosing to be either our own jailers or our own liberators. If we were less moved by the thought it would have less influence on us. A few examples might help to further illustrate what is meant by mentally holding on and letting go.

- We might experience considerable stress in maintaining or holding on to our self-image: the need to be right, the need to be liked all the time, the need to appear like we know more than we do. This can make it hard to acknowledge when we are wrong, to accept ourselves, or ask a question and seek help when we need it. It is strange that asking for help can seem like such a threatening situation.
- Later in life we might find ourselves trying to maintain a larger mortgage than we can service comfortably. We can find our lives being ruled by it.
- We can hold on to a role in life long after it has passed and feel unable, or at least unwilling, to let it go. As a result we can be unable to flow with the inevitable changes in life. We might quietly acknowledge that we should let it go and move on, but there is another part of us which will not let it go, no matter how much difficulty it causes.
- Another example might be holding on to plans. Unforeseen events occur almost every day and they can often interfere with our preconceived idea of how the day should go. If we remain fixed to this preconceived idea it will be very difficult for us to flow with events and adjust happily as daily events unfold. All our flexibility is sacrificed and we become apprehensive and rigid.
- Letting go also means knowing when to stop—whether it be eating, talking, working, exercising, playing or anything else. Although one part of ourselves knows we need to stop or move on there is often a contrary part of us that will not let go.
- Language is very informative about this very principle; as an example consider what happens when we hold onto an

opinion tightly. Doesn't conflict or a tug-of-war arise easily when people hold opposite points of view? As a result don't we sometimes lose sight of an issue when we become embroiled in the competition to prove who is right and who is wrong? Don't we often feel threatened or worthless when our opinion is challenged or defeated? But instead can't opinions be stood back from and examined in an objective and cooperative fashion without stress and conflict, so that it ceases to be 'my opinion' and just becomes 'an opinion.' As such we can enjoy more fruitful discussions instead of competitions. Don't we maintain much more equilibrium, stability and objectivity in this way?

Ideas are just ideas, but we often attribute so much to them. It is the very fact that we have staked some sort of personal claim over them that they seem to be 'me' and 'mine'. This personalising things makes many situations threatening and upsets the flow of life.

> **'An enlightened being is one who does not resist the flow of life, but keeps moving with it.'**
> —*Fritjof Capra,* The Tao of Physics

As we become more aware of where tension and unhappiness is coming from we will start to see that what we are able to let go of, rather than what we hold on to, is more important in determining how free, spontaneous and happy we feel. Furthermore, it liberates us to be more responsive to the needs of others.

Our growing ability to let it go soon teaches us that it feels very natural to feel at ease, although it may not be a common experience. It is a little like coming home. When we let go of it all for a little while we may note that it is the stress that is not natural although it is common, and peace of mind is natural although it is not common. Stress, if you like, has become 'second nature'—it has become habitual. In time we discover that peacefulness and calmness is our 'first nature.' This is less obvious to us when we are young and are still in the process of developing the habits we will have to live with for the rest of our lives. It is far easier to develop better habits sooner rather than later.

When under stress we can get pre-occupied with 'how much can I get' or 'what am I missing out on'. Sometimes it is good to challenge our habitual thought patterns with a question such as 'How much can I do without?', which was posed by Socrates.

Life, if we allow it to, can become an endless and restless chase for happiness by trying to get what we don't have, holding on to what we've got, or mourning for what we have lost. Though having certain things can sometimes be very enjoyable, circumstances determine that we must go without them at other times. If we are able to let go when we should or must then we feel more secure and at peace in the midst of any given situation.

Letting go doesn't mean giving everything up, just the mental attachment to it. It also doesn't mean becoming inert; on the contrary, it is generally the hold of an idea, fear or limitation that prevents us from acting purposefully and spontaneously when we need to. Letting go also doesn't mean 'anything goes', it simply means acting freely, without tension or compulsion. If you find yourself doing something unreasonable, try to observe what is being held on to. Letting go does not mean not acting. If the thought really is a useful one then by all means act on it, but the choice to act or not act can only come in the freedom from compulsion.

Furthermore, letting go does not mean fighting with ourselves or suppressing something. The tension that arises from this 'internal fight' comes when we are holding on to two opposing ideas or wants at the same time. One can look objectively at them and decide to let go of what is unhelpful or unwise according to our best judgement. Later, if it becomes apparent that we made a mistake, there is no need to criticise ourself but there may be a need to learn from the experience. Learning and moving on is another important aspect of letting go.

It seems paradoxical but we gain self-control and equilibrium not by using more force, but by using less. This is why feeling truly self-controlled always involves a relaxed state. It takes place by enlisting a little wisdom and applying a little reason. Being unable to let go is a huge source of frustration, insecurity and loss of self-control to us, because it places us at the influence of prevailing circumstances. It is getting hooked that leaves us so open to manipulation.

Acceptance

There is a prayer, sometimes called the Serenity Prayer. It includes the following three principles:

- The ability to accept the things one must accept
- The strength to change the things that one should change
- The wisdom to tell the difference

A closely related principle in managing stress better is acceptance. Things are not always the way we would like them to be—in fact generally they are not. They are, at least for now, the way they are. Many things in life cannot be changed—at least not in the short term. Consider how learning to accept can alleviate stress. It can transform a problem into a non-problem by a simple change of attitude. We may not be able to control the problem, but we can control the attitude. Sometimes we have to suffer things the way they are.

> '(Suffering well is) nothing but a willingness to suffer what you have to suffer, even if you do not wish to. Unless you suffer willingly, you will certainly suffer unwillingly; and unless you allow yourself to be led, you will be seized and violently dragged away. . . . He who suffers well turns what is bad for him into good.'
> —*Marsilio Ficino*

When we accept situations that we previously refused to accept, or accept what it will take to deal with them, we experience major releases of stress and increases in effective action. To refuse to accept is to ignore the obvious, which, of course, does not make the problem go away. With the peace of mind that follows acceptance the mind is in a far more effective state to act. We can find a new resourcefulness and courage that can be used to deal much more effectively with our situation. Denial and non-acceptance consumes an enormous amount of energy and achieves nothing useful.

Acceptance is not an excuse for inaction. It may be that we need to wait or it may be that we need to act. If we are lost in the forest we have to accept that we are lost and with care and attention start taking our bearings. It does not mean that we will stay there. Things may be the way they are for good reason. Who knows?

'To some people surrender may have negative connotations, implying defeat, giving up, failing to rise to the challenges of life, becoming lethargic, and so on. True surrender, however, is something entirely different. It does not mean to passively put up with whatever situation you find yourself in and to do nothing about it. Nor does it mean to cease making plans or initiating positive action. Surrender is the simple but profound wisdom of *yielding to* rather than opposing the flow of life. The only place where you can experience the flow of life is the Now, so to surrender is to accept the present moment unconditionally and without reservation.'
—*Eckhart Tolle,* The Power of Now

Practice for the week: *During day-to-day life when you notice stress or conflict, whether it be internal or external, see what is being held on to. Is the tension related to holding an opinion, a condition for happiness we have set up in our own minds, a fear, a criticism of oneself or another, a like or dislike or a desire that might not be prudent. See what effect holding on has, and what effect it has on the stress if we let go of the mental tension. What effect does it have on stress if we willingly accept things that we can't or shouldn't change or if we accept the effort it takes to change the things we should?*

Task 3: Presence of mind

> 'Are you stressed? Are you so busy getting to the future that
> the present is reduced to a means of getting there? Stress is
> caused by being 'here' but wanting to be 'there', or being in the
> present but wanting to be in the future. It's a split that tears
> you apart inside.'
> —*Eckhart Tolle,* The Power of Now

Living in the present is alluded to by common terms like
'presence of mind', meaning that someone was able to see clearly
what was happening in a difficult situation and to do exactly
what was needed to be done. Interestingly, in such situations of
high performance people also generally experience being quite
calm. 'Absent minded', on the other hand, suggests that the mind
is in some other place or time. This is hardly a condition
for effective action or understanding. The result of absent-
mindedness is that we lose touch with the reality of the present
situation and either don't respond at all or respond to the imaginary situation instead of the actual one. Either way we do not
meet it effectively. This is certainly a recipe for increasing stress
and complication.

**Paradox 9: The present moment is safe. Dreams
about past and future can be like a dark forest in
which we get lost.**

You may have noticed during the mindfulness exercise how
often the mind is full of thoughts about the past and future.
While thinking about the past we can replay old events, fill the
mind with regrets, keep re-experiencing old hurts, criticising
ourselves for old mistakes and so on. Such thoughts go round
and round in ever-decreasing circles. Thinking about the future
we can imagine many problems that will never happen, experi-

ence anxiety and fear, or have very rigid ideas about how things should turn out. We can prejudice situations and conversations and then feel frustrated because things don't go according to a pre-conceived idea. All this projecting into the past and future that goes on unconsciously and habitually is disabling in the present.

Being in the present does not in any way preclude constructive and purposeful forethought and planning. Planning is an entirely necessary part of daily living. Worrying about the outcome is not. Preparing for a future exam is useful. Fear of failure is not. Conscious planning and preparation is all we can do. The event will unfold in its own time. Being in the here and now is something we rarely practise, and often avoid. Living for the here and now does not mean not caring about the future, or having no constructive and responsible plans. By paying more attention to the here and now we are more able to respond to events and people as they arise in daily life without prejudice (pre-judgement). We can let events unfold naturally and without tension and just see what happens. We can treat it like an experiment. Part of this experiment will be attending to one job at a time as they become priorities. If it happens that we need to adjust our priorities over time then we can practise flowing with it.

When the mind is intent on imaginary future losses and gains it loses sight of the actual thoughts and motives that are driving us here and now. Put another way, concern about the ends frequently blinds us to the means, and if the means are not correct then the end will never be attained, or if it is it will not produce the expected effect. Concern for the future that makes us miss the present manifests in many other ways also.

- If our mind is full of imagining what we are going to do when we arrive at work, we are likely to take our mind's eye off the road and take a wrong turn, or have a crash and not arrive at all.

- We can get so preoccupied about an exam in the future that we find it hard to study effectively and efficiently, which we need to do now in order to prepare for the exam.
- We can get so anxious about the outcome of an interview that we can't focus effectively on it.
- An athlete such as a cricketer can be so concerned with scoring a century that he experiences the 'nervous nineties' or goes out because he lost his concentration and missed the ball. Keeping the eye on the ball is another way of saying 'be mindful'.
- We can get so caught up worrying and thinking about the hundred jobs we will have to do that we become very inefficient and exhausted. How many times have we awoken in the morning and felt exhausted just thinking about the day ahead? Well, what is this 'day ahead of us?' It is only a picture in the mind, and it hasn't even happened.
- Notice how we can keep replaying past unpleasant conversations with someone or some past negative experience and feel so stressed by the very thought of them that we avoid them whenever we can.

Is escapism an answer? An appropriate time out like relaxing or taking a walk, going on a holiday or seeing a movie can be very useful to help refresh us, but although escapism seems an attractive option it can cause more problems than it is worth. The more we fail to deal with the here and now, the grimmer situations can become and the more we lose our confidence in our ability to cope with them. When our situations are neglected we do not release our burden—we merely carry it around with us like a millstone. Like avoiding a fine, it only tends to attract interest. It doesn't go away. We can get into a vicious circle of stress and avoidance. Often our attempts to avoid present responsibilities are because of an artificial idea about our own lack of ability or a distorted idea of the largeness of the task, but we can reverse this process.

Practice for the week: *Practise living in the here and now by practising 'presence of mind' rather than 'absent mindedness'. By all means prioritise tasks, but focus on the one task that is relevant at any given time. When stressed observe whether day-dreaming and imagining about the future and past can fill the mind with fears, anxieties, shattered expectations, grief, remorse and distractions. Do they disable and distract us from effectively dealing with the present? If mistakes are made, try to recall what the mind was preoccupied with at the time. Was it on the present? Use the senses such as touch, sight or hearing to help engage the mind in the present and see what effect that has.*

Task 4: Limitations

'Our deepest fear is not that we are inadequate. Our deepest
fear is that we are powerful beyond measure. It is our light not
our darkness that most frightens us. . . . As we are liberated
from our own fear our presence automatically liberates
others.'
—*Nelson Mandela,* 1994 Inauguration Speech

Through the mindfulness exercise and the practising of Tasks 1
to 3 you would have begun to gain an appreciation that when the
distracted and wasteful mental activity begins to quieten down
something else starts to naturally arise:

- Psychological and physical peace arises as tension
  dissipates, giving the potential for our thoughts and actions
  to be more free, and unhindered.
- We feel spontaneously lighter and happier in ourselves.
- Our natural intelligence and problem-solving ability has
  more possibility of functioning.
- Communication is more focused, natural and connected.

In this task we are still practising letting go, but in particular we
are applying it to letting go of limitations. There are two basic
types of limitations. One is stress-laden, inhibiting, unreasonable and habitual and the other is stress-reducing, reasonable
and conscious. We will examine each of these in turn with the
aim of dispensing with the former and encouraging the latter.

Firstly we will consider the stress-laden form of limitations.
If we were asked what our limitations were we might be hard
pressed to say exactly what they were. We could approach the
issue in another way. If we asked ourselves 'have we reached our
full potential?' the answer would surely be 'no'. Why don't we
realise our potential for happiness and fulfilment in work, at
home or in relationships? What inhibits our ability and enjoy-

ment in learning and other areas of our lives? Why are so many situations stressful and burdensome before we have even undertaken them? Why do we habitually procrastinate and put some things off and totally avoid other things? How resilient can we really be when meeting the stresses of every-day life? How much potential do we have that is untapped?

Interestingly, the Latin word for education (educare) means 'to draw out'. It means that the potential lies within but needs to be drawn out, or uncovered. What covers it? Well, we might observe what happens when we are presented with a situation like being asked to sing, draw, cook, operate a computer or some other activity. There are a few activities that we enjoy and readily perform but for the rest there often immediately arises a long conditioned prejudicial idea like 'I can't sing', or 'I can't draw'. These ideas have been picked up and reinforced for many years, probably since we were young children. What is the effect of them? We can observe this for ourselves, but we might have noticed an increase of tension, fear, avoidance behaviour, embarrassment or a half-hearted attempt from which we learn little and derive precious little enjoyment. Contrast this to the spontaneous response of a young child who is offered the opportunity to sing, draw, cook or learn about computers. For the young child there is interest, attention, enjoyment and learning. It does not take long, however, for this spontaneous and open response to become covered.

Tapping this potential will depend on how much it is covered or uncovered. Limitations can take many different forms and have a variety of effects. These self-imposed limitations are only as fixed as we believe them to be. We subject ourselves to them, but we also tend to project them onto others. Observing them and then practising intelligently confronting them is the way to slowly show ourselves that they are generally self-imposed ideas we hold about ourselves like habitual patterns of thought, reinforced over many years. The trouble is that the more they are reinforced, the more fixed they become. The opportunity is that the more they are ignored the less fixed they become.

Limitations take many forms. They can include ideas such as 'this work practice can't be changed', or 'I could never speak in public', or 'I'm too unintelligent to understand mathematics', or 'I'm a nervy person'. They can be habits such as 'I always drive fast', or 'this job must be done the same way every time', or likes and dislikes such as 'I like Italian food, but hate Brussels sprouts'. We often limit a response with an assumption about how one should feel or respond to a given situation. In meeting some form of adversity, consider, for example, the implications of a statement like 'you must feel devastated by such and such'. One could always ask oneself 'why must I?' Does that mean that one mustn't cope or one mustn't transcend it? Similarly, with a lack of success we often hear 'you must feel devastated about failing', as if it would be pathological to see it as a learning or character-building experience. Such thoughts are being taken on and rehearsed without us being aware of it and they can rule large sections of our lives.

> **'If you can meet with triumph and disaster,**
> **And treat those two imposters just the same.'**
> —*Rudyard Kipling*, 'If'

We have these ideas unconsciously going on in our minds all day long, not only making us stressed but also confining our actions. By testing them we can demonstrate to ourselves that these state-ments above are as true as we believe them to be. The longer and more passionately they have been believed, the longer and more vehemently they tend to hang on. Better never to take them on in the first place.

One needs to be realistic, however, and acknowledge that some people do tend to have more natural aptitude in particular areas than others. We may also acknowledge that if we are not practised in something then we may have a great deal to learn, whether it be about singing, drawing, cooking or anything else. It will require practise. It may also be appropriate to take on a limitation safe step by safe step. If one has a fear of high places it might not be appropriate to jump off a cliff with a hang glider in one go. The point is not to ignore the limitation but rather to deal with it in a graded and responsible manner. This will make it far easier to deal with the stress and inhibiting effect of these limitations when needs and opportunities present themselves to us in daily life. If there is no need to confront a limitation then it will not cause us much stress or inconvenience. If there is a need to take something on then it is far better to take it on without a whole set of negative ideas about ourselves and the task. Better to give the attention to the task and not the ideas.

When the environment seeks to confront us with one of our assumed limitations we may notice a feeling of stress or a feeling of being closed in. The stress can be alleviated by letting go of the thought and then exercising a choice in what to give our attention to: the limiting thought or the situation that has presented itself to us. Daily life doesn't necessarily move within the confines of our thinking, so it is much better to realise that we have the potential to be able to adjust our thoughts and behaviour to meet the needs of situations as they arise in daily life. If left unexamined these limitations prevent us from learning, coping, being spontaneous, experiencing or improvising. Some of them have been deeply held and believed for a long time and these may take some time to go; therefore it may be better to start with what are apparently small or insignificant limitations first and build up. The important thing is to appreciate the process and get on with it.

Setting reasonable limits.

The word limitations can have other connotations. Above we have been discussing the unreasonable and often stress-laden ones. There are, of course, reasonable limits to set in daily life, for example, finding the appropriate limits in our lifestyle. This includes limiting how much we eat, drink, work or exercise.

'Nothing too much.' (also often translated as 'moderation in all things.')
—*Ancient Greek saying*

Too little or too much of anything can be unhealthy and lead to stress and illness. Letting go of limitations is not an encouragement to live life to excess or to do the things that our better judgement tells us are unsafe or illegal. These are two entirely different uses of the word. The only way to be aware of what these appropriate limits are is to pay attention in the present and see what the situation requires. Some limitations can save us a lot of discomfort and expense. This topic will be dealt with in more detail in the self-discipline task.

Paradox 10: More is not necessarily better when it comes to most things in life.

Practice for the week: *When situations arise in daily life, observe the tendency for habitual limitations to also arise. See what effect they have and how they can prejudice events. If appropriate and reasonable, observe the effect of confronting a limitation or fixed idea about oneself by letting it go and practising paying attention to the situation instead. By all means seek help if need be. Are these limitations self-imposed and not fixed? This task will require you to be unconcerned about success or failure and instead to just have a go.*

Task 5: Listening

Listening is a crucial skill—one that we need to examine. Firstly, when practising mindfulness it does not take us long to discover that we spend a lot of time listening to a great deal of mental chatter. This happens unconsciously, whether we want it to or not. It is also obvious that problems in communication between individuals and groups are the source of much stress. They produce alienation, conflict and loneliness. Effective communication, which begins with listening, breaks down barriers between people and resolves conflict.

But this is only half the story. It is not just a matter of whether we are listening to others effectively; it is also a matter of what we are listening to within ourselves. Do we listen to our intuition? Do we get caught up with endlessly listening to a whole lot of negative thoughts? Shakespeare dramatically represented this choice we have in his plays. In one tragedy, Othello, the hero listens to the wrong thing and thus makes some very poor choices. He listens to Iago who spellbinds Othello, making untruth appear true and truth appear untrue. He suggests we cannot find tranquility or contentment until we see things the right way up again.

'Oh, now forever farewell the tranquil mind, farewell content.'
—*Othello*

How effective is our listening and what are we listening to? Even if our occupation involves listening for large parts of the day, our listening is often less effective than it could be. How many times have we noticed the following?

- While in a conversation we hardly heard a word of what the other person was saying.
- We asked a question and didn't hear the answer or told someone something and it is as if they didn't hear what we were saying.

- We were introduced to someone and immediately forgot their name as if we had never heard it.
- Have we ever noticed that if we hold a strong opinion we find it difficult to hear the other person's point of view without a barrage of objections going on inside our minds?
- Do we ever find ourselves in a distracted state listening to a stream of negative thoughts or self-criticsm?

These are examples of unmindfulness. In such cases we are generally listening to the conversation we are having in our own thoughts rather than the person in front of us. This mental noise or chatter takes many forms such as day-dreams, anticipated conversations or even music that just plays and plays in the mind. Internal conversations can be mundane ideas like 'what am I going to eat when I get home?', or ideas about what the other person is saying such as 'they don't know what they are talking about' or 'I'm right and you're wrong', or comments about ourselves and our abilities such as 'I hope I understand the answer' or 'what impression am I making?'

It is obvious that the more we listen to the thinking or chatter inside the mind the less able we are to listen in a clear and unbiased way to the people and events around us. It is also obvious that we can actually generate enormous amounts of stress out of nothing by doing this. Next time we are stressed, angry or fearful, for example, notice what conversation we are listening to in our thoughts. Observe this mental chatter. That will begin to break the spell. When the mind is distracted in this way it is generally reinforcing a whole stream of habitual or negative thoughts about ourselves or others. Notice also the effects of leaving the chatter and bringing our attention back to the present moment through listening. Though we might be listening to a whole stream of negative thoughts about ourselves, connecting with the sense of hearing may alert us to the fact that there are birds, people, cars and a whole world outside. It takes us out of the imaginary world, which appears attractive and fulfilling, but which in the end proves to be anything but.

Sometimes we neglect to listen to what others say, and sometimes we neglect to listen to what we are saying ourselves. Listening more attentively to what comes out of our own mouths can also be very informative. This sort of endless internal conversation and chatter might only be obvious, or at least be most obvious, while practising the mindfulness exercise.

Listening mindfully, when considered in its broadest sense, means more than just hearing words. It includes an awareness of what goes on under the surface such as the body language and emotional state of a person. Put another way, what is subtly being communicated is generally more informative than the words. Even though a person may not say much, if we are attentive we can understand an enormous amount about what their needs, feelings and grievances are, and in the process become more helpful, compassionate, resolute or conciliatory as needed. When our own thoughts are cluttered or prejudicing the conversation we do not pick up much of what is happening beneath the surface. Furthermore, we are unable to hear our own intuition, which tends to speak quietly, even without words. This issue will be examined in more detail in the self-discipline task.

It is not too difficult to observe the spiral of conflict that arises from a breakdown in listening. When conversations take place without much listening then we tend to speak louder and more aggressively, or maybe we cut off altogether. The other person may respond to the loudness and aggressiveness by speaking in the same manner or cutting off also. Thus we arrive at a no win situation. This can be observed as readily in the dealings between countries as it can be in the dealings of individuals. If we make an effort to listen carefully, openly and sincerely then the opposite has the potential to occur, which helps to resolve hostility and stress. When we listen to others more attentively we generally find that the listening is reciprocated.

There are two things that we can experiment with to help facilitate good listening and thereby better communication. First, we need to recognise that we are always listening to something but, as we may have observed, like Othello, we often find ourselves listening to an imaginary conversation in the mind, which prevents us from listening to the reality of what is actually happening. If we find this chatter in the mind diverting our attention from who or what is in front of us, we can experiment with turning the attention away from it, as we do with the mindfulness exercise. We don't have to feed it with attention if we choose. This can be very effectively done through hearing, which is of course one of the five senses. When attention is connected with what is really going on in this way, the mind is prevented from getting caught up with its habitual activity and self-talk . Hence we have the term 'coming to our senses'. This is nothing more than being in touch with reality again.

Next we need to remember the principle of letting go—that is, letting go of our preconceived and rehearsed ideas about how conversations should go, which just serve to prejudice (prejudge) events. Experiment with letting the process of communication be a cooperative and spontaneous inquiry.

Practice for the week: *What are we listening to? For how much of the day are we 'away with the birds' distracted by self-talk and internal conversations? What is the nature and effect of this pattern of thought? As an experiment, practise listening less to the chatter and conversations that go on in our minds by listening more fully to what is going on around us: family, friends and work-mates. Note the effect of this. When stressed, note down the sorts of things that you are listening to in your mind.*

Task 6: Self-discipline

> **Paradox 11: Avoiding a need consumes more energy than meeting it.**

Why is it that putting necessary things off doesn't allow us to really relax even when we choose to do things we like instead? Have we noticed how we are often at loggerheads with ourselves about various issues and decisions? What is going on when we feel like we are fighting with ourselves or sabotaging ourselves?

Occasionally we become aware that we are unable to do what we need to do, not so much due to external restrictions on our behaviour, but because of internal restriction. For example, it is often hard to get ourselves motivated, or hard to stop something when we need to. When these internal restrictions and conflicts are holding sway do we not feel burdened and constrained?

'Discipline' is a word we often associate with oppression and constraint. 'Freedom' is a word that we often associate with doing what we like and stress-free living, but perhaps things are not always the way they seem.

> **Paradox 12: True freedom is attained through the *intelligent* application of self-discipline. A lack of discipline is not a free or happy state.**

To consider why this may be so we have to take into consideration that there are different aspects of ourselves, different motivations that are not all of equal wisdom. This obvious and yet easily overlooked fact has been written about for thousands of years.

> 'There are among men several sorts of reasonings, good and
> bad. Admire them not too easily and reject them not either, but
> if any falsehoods be advanced give way with mildness and
> arm thyself with patience.'
> —*Pythagoras,* The Golden Verses

Self-discipline suggests that some part of ourselves is disciplining another part. For example, if we look at ourselves we will note that there is a more reasonable part and a more irresponsible part. Similarly, with the emotions we might notice a more positive and compassionate part and a darker part. For want of a better term we could describe the aspects of reason and positive emotion as our 'better judgement' and unreasonableness and negative emotion as our 'lesser judgement'. Living with considerably less stress is largely a matter of the better judgement being able to exercise rightful and moderating control and authority over our lesser judgement. The better judgement is constituted by reason or rationality. The lesser judgement is usually constituted by a number of things, but most commonly by strong desires, aversions, inappropriate and outdated habits, unreasonable beliefs, whims, and misguided emotions. This is all clutter in the mind that becomes increasingly obvious after a few weeks of practising the mindfulness exercises. It is also the stuff around which our internal chatter tends to revolve. Better judgement, on the other hand, tends to work quietly and bases its decisions on a clear and broad view of events as opposed to the restless and vocal 'egging on' of our lesser judgement. There are many examples of this, such as procrastination, avoidance and overdoing things.

- Have we ever noticed that the house can be in dire need of a clean but we can't bring ourselves to do it? Do we feel at ease by avoiding it? What happens when we get on with something that you have been putting off? Do we not feel freer and like a burden has been lifted from our shoulders?

- When studying, have we ever felt extremely stressed, recognising that exams are near, but find ourselves unable to do the required study? Once the study is begun do we not feel much better?
- Have we ever noted the need to spend some time with the family or have some leisure time but can't tear ourselves away from work? Is it not hard to find that right balance?
- Have we ever noticed that 'quiet knowing' when we have had enough to eat or drink but that little voice that comes in immediately after, saying, 'oh it won't hurt just to have some more'? Have we noticed the indigestion, lethargy or hangover that tends to follow?
- Have we noticed how our mind can give a thousand excuses to avoid practising something which is good for us, like the mindfulness meditation, and a thousand justifications for practising something which is bad for us like worrying?

In these commonplace examples is it not a paradox that doing what we want to do and putting off what we need to do doesn't lead to ease or happiness, whereas forgoing what we want until we have attended to what we need to do lets us rest more easily and stress-free? Only if we are able to discipline ourselves to do whatever we think is best are we able to truly choose. No discipline means no freedom. The result of being unable to do what we think best is that we can't avoid feeling stressed and confined. Self-discipline often requires a certain amount of strength and courage. It is brought about by learning to *let go* of that which is of no use, *not by using force and certainly not by self-criticism.* It requires regular practise, but as the practise takes place, like strengthening a muscle, we get stronger. Contrary to our ideas about discipline, reasonable use of discipline actually leads to freedom, not suppression, and peace, not tension. Effort may initially be required, but soon what was difficult becomes easier.

The best form of self-discipline is a relaxed and spontaneous response to the needs of a situation, not getting embroiled in a court-room battle in our heads about whether we are good or bad. It has much to do with being in the present —when we recognise something in the moment we follow it. Plato put it in these terms when he described the state of inner harmony that is associated with responsible action the word used to carry this sense was 'just':

> 'The just man does not permit the several elements within him to interfere with one another, or any of them to do the work of others; he sets in order his own inner life, and is his own master, and his own law, and at peace with himself; and when he has bound the three principles within him, which may be compared to the higher (reason), lower (appetite) and middle (passion) notes of the scale ...'
>
> —*Plato,* The Republic

We could use lifestyle factors such as smoking, physical exercise, or drinking alcohol as a way of illustrating further. Many of the things that we want are not good for us, and some of the things we wish to avoid are good for us. Many things are good to a point and then are bad in excess. There is a part of the mind which does know *good*, *bad* and appropriate measure, but we are not well practised in listening to it and heeding it. Some things of course, are good or healthy or enjoyable to a point but then unhealthy beyond that point. Being self-disciplined does not mean not enjoying things, or always going without, or always working. It does not, however, mean a cold and joyless austerity either.

> 'Dost though think, because thou art virtuous, there shall be no more cakes and ale?'
>
> —*Shakespeare,* Twelfth Night II, *ii*

In its best sense it is not about someone always telling us what to do and when to stop. It is best if we develop this quiet knowing from within ourselves. If our upbringing has not acquainted us with it, or habitually encouraged us to ignore it, then we will obviously have a bit of practise to do.

Discipline also sometimes means atoning for something, correcting a mistake or apologising. One very common reason for experiencing continuing stress is that we don't always make appropriate correction when we should. It is always best to atone, correct the mistake or apologise as soon as possible if this is what our better judgement tells us. It is like following our conscience. If we are not sure if this is best we can simply try an experiment. Avoid it and see whether the mind finds some peace and rest. Then do it and see how what effect this has on the mind and emotions. We may find that it is not possible to relieve stress while carrying out and repeating actions that go against the grain of our better nature.

'How use doth breed a habit in a man!'
—*Shakespeare,* Two Gentlemen of Verona, V, iv

There is a simple law of nature: what we practise we get good at. This is both a blessing and a curse, because we can condition both good and bad ways of doing things. We call these 'habits'. Sometimes it is very obvious that we feel compelled to do things that we ought not to do or would rather not do. Some habits and compulsions can be quite strong and unhelpful to ourselves and others, which can involve much stress. Habits can take a little effort to change, but mindfulness can be a great facilitator of change. One pre-requisite, however, is that we actually do want to be free of the habit and are not just kidding ourselves and others. If we persevere there are a number of stages and more than a little patience involved in the process. These stages are as follows:

1. Begin by dropping the self-criticism around the habit.
2. Become conscious of the action when it is playing out. Just watch it.
3. Observe the anticipation behind it that is built upon mental images from the past, and projected into the future.
4. Observe the effects of the habit, how it leaves us feeling and what it costs us in various ways.
5. If we wish to be free of it then begin to ride out the desire for whatever it is, like letting a wave go under us rather than fighting it. As in mindfulness, without hesitation keep letting the attention be gently directed from the mental images back to whatever we are doing.
6. Soon we will begin to notice that the habit begins to 'hollow out' and becomes a mere going through the motions as it has less and less compulsive force.
7. The habit becomes less frequent and there are longer and longer periods of freedom from it.
8. There are occasional short-lived relapses, but it is easier to get back on track.
9. The habit eventually has little or no hold on us.

It is important not to get too caught up on the success and failure of our efforts. Although it often looks like we are getting nowhere if we are making sincere efforts we are actually making progress although it may not be obvious initially. We had to fall off a bicycle many times before we found our balance. It is the same with developing self-discipline. We simply observe and practise. By practising discipline we can be more free and responsible in our actions. Our 'yes' means nothing unless we can just as easily say 'no'.

Practice for the week: *Observe the effects of too little self-discipline in things such as procrastination or overdoing something. Experiment with attending willingly and immediately to the needs of any given situation you encounter in the day and see what effect this has on stress. Is stress relieved when we don't put things off? Does it take more energy to put something off than to simply do it? Practise saying no a few times to the things we want to say no to.*

Task 7: Emotions

We have considered the principle of letting go over the previous tasks, but there is an area which requires special mention, and that is to do with emotional holding on. So often we habitually play on certain emotions no matter how much harm, division or discontent they may be causing to ourselves or others. Even when we do notice the effect of negative emotions we often replace one with another, like replacing anger with guilt or self-criticism.

Our negative emotions tend to overlay a quite natural disposition for the positive. When we let go of negative emotions we make space for the deeper, stronger and more useful emotions to arise. Sometimes, however, negative emotions can be quite strong and deep-seated and in extreme cases it is useful to seek specialised counselling to deal with them. Where there is some level of objectivity and motivation the emotions, negative or positive, can be observed just like the thoughts. As such we can develop a choice as to whether to go with them or not, remembering that those we hold onto will be the ones which control us. This does not imply suppression. Like a train pulling up to the station, you may not be able to stop the train coming in, but you can decide whether or not to get on it.

The negativity directed at ourselves or others takes many forms. Holding on to negative emotions such as resentment, fear, criticisms, guilt, blame and the rest leads to disunity, misery and conflict within ourselves and with others. If we examine these emotions closely and impartially we find that they are often based upon unreasonable thinking. When their unreasonableness and destructiveness is seen clearly they start to lose their influence over us.

A more positive emotional state does not necessarily equate with agreeing with everyone, being sickly-sweet to people, or being at the whim of everyone around us. There may be times when we need to confront an issue or stand up for a principle with courage, clarity and conviction. At these times fear may have to step aside so that courage can surface.

Each emotion can have its place—even something like anger. It is not always negative. Sometimes anger is appropriate in a given situation and to suppress it would be harmful. Appropriate anger, however, is quite different in nature to inappropriate anger. Appropriate anger is born of a clear perception of a situation, is not excessive in its use of force, lasts only as long as it is needed, and never has any venom or harmful intent in it or towards ourselves or others. We feel in control of it, not controlled by it and when the situation is over there is no residual anger taken from it. Inappropriate anger, on the other hand, is the opposite of all these things. It is born of a distorted or biased perception, is excessive, lasts long after the event and is harmful, not helpful. It tends to leave behind residual ill-feeling and the seeds for further problems and conflict. If we can be mindful enough, it is better to let go of it, which is no doubt difficult if it has been allowed to get up a head of steam over a long period. In day-to-day life inappropriate anger is far more common than appropriate anger.

There is nobody we punish more with the bad feelings we hold on to than ourselves, poisoning ourselves as it were. We also tend to take out our bad feelings on others, which is a maladaptive way of alleviating the unrest which we feel. Others in the same predicament as ourselves take them out on us and so the cycle continues. As the old saying goes, what we habitually give to others is eventually returned to us.

Regardless of our environment these negative feelings are often internally generated and tend to have their origins in the past. It is certainly hard for us to make positive changes while we are in an environment that constantly brings out more negative aspects of ourselves. We need to choose our environment when we can. Whether or not emotions are projected from others, we do have a choice as to whether we take them on.

Often, being ruled by the past, we replay unpleasant memories in the mind and continually re-experience deeply entrenched hostility and negativity, and thus the stress that inevitably goes with it. The way out of this predicament is to observe the state of the emotions, clear the mind of the past, and respond freshly and spontaneously with an open heart to the here and now. Holding onto the past never allows a fresh and healthier approach to eventuate.

Forgiveness and opening the heart is our own responsibility in that nobody else can do it for us. It would do well to be as careful of what we are giving as what we are getting. Now that we are gaining more insight into the things that have a hold on us, we will also naturally start to see that others are in the same predicament and quite possibly unaware of it. If we understand our own situation better we tend to become more understanding of others and thus compassion quite naturally begins to arise where there used to be anger.

Becoming aware of and undoing negative emotions can sometimes be a little challenging. This is one of the main reasons we often avoid waking up. Beware of entertaining self-criticism that tends to be destructive. Useful and objective self-evaluation is constructive, but criticism is very disabling and energy-sapping. It also slows learning and sabotages constructive change. This is one of the areas in which the power of group support can be most telling. We often find that what felt so private and personal is in fact shared with others.

Practice for the week: *Without self-recrimination, observe the effects of when we are ruled with negative emotions. See what the thought patterns behind negative emotions that arise in daily life are. Observe the effects of letting go of negative emotions such as fear, anger, resentment and guilt. See what the effect of letting go of the desire to play on or manipulate these emotions in others is.*

Task 8: Expanding self-interest

There is a very old but very informative teaching story which I first heard at school. It roughly goes as follows.

> A man asked his teacher to show him Heaven and Hell. His teacher agreed and inquired as to which the man would like to see first. The man said he wished to see hell first. He was duly transported to a beautiful mansion set amid the most magnificent and bountiful countryside. Entering the mansion the man was taken to a banquet hall of extraordinary opulence where there was spread out the most sumptuous feast he had ever laid eyes on. He quickly perceived, however, that the room was also filled with the most excruciating misery he had ever seen. Despite this opulence people were crying out piteously, sick with starvation. He wondered why this was so and, taking a closer look, he saw that the people were compelled to eat their food with forks which were four feet long, too long to get the food into their mouths. The man wondered who could have been so cruel as to play such a macabre joke on these poor souls. The man then asked to be taken to Heaven. His teacher dutifully took him to an identical mansion set in an identical countryside. On entering he was shown to an identical banquet hall with the same feast laid out that he had seen before. The man quickly saw that the people were also compelled to eat with the same four-foot forks and yet, to his surprise, everyone was healthy, happy and well-fed. Wondering why he again looked closely. There was only one difference he could see between Heaven and Hell. In Hell people starved because they could not feed themselves. In Heaven all were happy because they fed each other.

The old saying has it that 'no man (or woman) is an island', yet we often live our lives as though we were. Surprisingly, despite the number of people around us, it is increasingly common these days to feel isolated and lonely. We have all had the experience of being at a party or similar social event and feeling very alone. Conversely, many of us will have experienced being physically alone or isolated, perhaps in nature or when relaxing at home, and yet we felt quite at ease and anything but lonely. It may be that loneliness or our level of connection to what or who is around us is more a state of mind than it is to do with our physical environment.

Paradox 13: We can feel lonely in company and at one with ourselves in solitude.

Also apparent, and perhaps not unrelated, is the observation that competition, rather than cooperation, is becoming far more the norm whether it be on the sporting field, in school or the business world. This can often be associated with inefficiency, conflict and insecurity. Healthy, good-spirited competition can be beneficial, but the spirit in which competition is taking place these days seems to be anything but good-spirited. Which sporting team is more successful and enjoyable to play in, the one with team spirit or where individuals play for themselves only? Which business or economic system tends to thrive in the longer run? One where 'greed is good'? Obviously not. This is the kind of thinking upon which economic collapses and litigation are based.

'Happiness is a byproduct of an effort to make someone else happy.'
—*Greta Brooker Palmer*

Paradox 14: In giving we receive.

It is easy enough to forget that our own well-being is inextricably linked with the well-being of those around us, whether it be on the community or international scale. To use an analogy, consider the body as a single and unified whole. It is made up of many individual cells formed into communities and groups, which we call organs, each of which has specific functions. Just as the overall health of the body relies on every individual part functioning well and happily, so too does the health of families, communities and countries. A cell that only has its own interests in mind is what we call a cancer cell. Acknowledging that there is an underlying unity and connectedness between people does not mean that everyone should be the same. It just acknowledges that underlying the diversity is a more essential unity.

Looked at in this light it seems that there may be reason in old adages like 'treating one's neighbour as oneself' because, in a manner of speaking, we and our neighbours are a part of the same Self. To ignore this simple truth would be to harm ourselves every bit as much as we potentially harm our neighbour.

A fair objection is often raised when considering this principle of caring for others, and that is that one can find one's generosity abused or that one looks after others so much that one's own needs are not met. Serving others does not mean ignoring the need to extend the same care to ourselves as we do to others. Expanding self-interest is not an exhortation to become a 'doormat' for other people to walk over. Pandering to selfishness, complacency or laziness would not be kind to ourselves or to others.

With these provisos considered, when we get into a very negative stress spiral we may have also noticed that we tend to get more and more ego-centred and our view of the world gets smaller and smaller. Individual interest, in the sense of isolation or separateness, easily comes at the expense of regard for others and is indeed based on a limited perception of the world. The desire for happiness is universal, and so it is understandable that if we feel something lacking in ourselves we try to relieve it by acquiring those things that we believe will fill it, even if this is at the expense of those around us. Preoccupation with self, as understandable as it is, unfortunately all-too-readily cuts us off from those around us.

Our experience soon indicates to us that stress is commonly associated with being cut off from or at loggerheads with others. Conversely, we may also have noted that we often have major releases in stress when we become more attentive to the needs of others. This also accords with the well-observed and documented phenomenon that times of crisis are often associated with far better mental health than times of plenty, when preoccupation with self tends to abound. Certainly one would find it preferable to learn the principle without having to go through a crisis, but even if that is what it takes then it is still a lesson well learned.

If we feel as if we are battling everyone and everyone is battling us then how could we feel anything but stressed and tired? If we asked ourselves, 'Would we survive more happily and effectively on a life raft where people looked after each other or one where it was every person for him or herself?' the answer would be obvious. Well, this consideration is of little use unless we test it in practise and see what happens to our own and other's stress. This sort of truism is not just a nicety, but is a principle of immense practical importance.

What are the barriers which stop this being put into practice and by what simple principles can these barriers and conflicts be broken down? The principles have all been covered in previous tasks: perception, letting go and acceptance, being in the present, listening, self-discipline and stepping over negative emotions. This task examines the effect of enlarging our view from the claustrophobic small-self or 'ego boundary' to include those around us, whether it be the family, workplace, community, nation and so on. There is no need to find some highly altruistic path to follow. We can start where we are by simply experimenting with the principle in our daily life as it arises. Considering the domestic, economic and environmental stresses that we currently face as a community, this principle has a wide-ranging and practical application.

Practice for the week: *Focusing on being practical and not merely idealistic, examine whether our view of self becomes isolated and cut off from others when we are stressed. Reflect on your ideas about self interest by expanding our sense of self to increasingly include those around us. Examine what effect this has on stress. Do we help ourselves at the same time as we help others? See what effect an act or gesture of kindness, care or goodwill has on our stress. Without trying to manufacture any particular effect, see what effect this has on others.*

Conclusion

The mindfulness principles and practices that have been discussed in this book are a beginning. We may consider them more
of a signpost than a destination. Put another way, they can
become a way of life the more we practise and understand them.
Over time we make steady progress even though there will be
peaks and troughs along the way. Many insights will be gained,
and yet still many questions will be unresolved. These questions
may find answers in future self-exploration. This is how it
should be. As we progress we may well eventually find that,
through living mindfully, 'the examined life is truly worth
living.'

Much of our confusion about stress and the things we value
in life are due to the fact that we do not know ourselves.

Paradox 15: *Knowing oneself is the first thing.
Without knowing our Self first we cannot and will
not truly understand the nature of stress, nor can we
attain the lasting happiness or freedom which we
are searching for.*

References

1 Watkins A. Mind-body Medicine: a clinician's guide to psycho-neuroimmunology. London: Churchill Livingstone, 1997.

2 Ader R., Cohen N., Felten D. Psychoneuroimmunology: interactions between the nervous system and the immune system. Lancet 1995; 345(8942):99-103.

3 Miller M., Rahe R. Life changes scaling for the 1990's. J Psychosom Res 1997;43(3):279-92.

4 Astin J. Why patients use alternative medicine: results of a national study. JAMA 1998;279(19):1548-53.

5 Kesterton J. Metabolic rate, respiratory exchange ratio and apnoeas during meditation. American J of Physiology 1989;256(3):632-8.

6 Benson H. The relaxation response and norepinephrine: a new study illuminates mechanisms. Australian J of Clinical Hypnotherapy and Hypnosis 1989;10(2):91-6.

7 Mills P., Schneider R., Hill D. et al. Beta-adrenergic receptor sensitivity in subjects practicing TM. J Psychosomatic Research 1990; 34(1):29-33.

8 Delmonte M. 'Physiological responses during meditation and rest.' Biofeedback and Self-regulation 1984;9(2):181-200.

9 Bagga O., Gandhi A., Bagga S. A study of the effect of TM and yoga on blood glucose, lactic acid, cholesterol and total lipids. J of Clinical Chemistry and Clinical Biochemistry 1981;19(8):607-8.

10 Echenhofer F., Coombs M. 'A brief review of research and controversies in EEG biofeedback and meditation.' The Journal of Transpersonal Psychology 1987;19(2):161-71.

11 Deepak K. et al. Meditation improves clinico-electroencephalographic measures in drug-resistant epileptics. Biofeedback and self-regulation 1994;19:(1)25-40.

12 Bujatti M. et al. 'Serotonin, noradrenaline, dopamine metabolites in TM technique.' Journal of Neural Transmission. 1976;39:257-67.

13 Jevning R., Anand R., Biedebach M. et al. Effects on regional cerebral blood flow of TM. Physiology and Behaviour 1996;59(3): 399-402.

14 Werner O. et al. 'Long-term endocrine changes in subjects practicing the TM and TM-siddhi program.' Psychosomatic Medicine 1986; 48(1-2):59-65.

15 Jedrczak A. et al. 'The TM-siddhi program, age, and brief tests of perceptual motor speed and non-verbal intelligence.' Journal of Clinical Psychology 1986;42(1):161-4.

16 Brown D. et al. 'Visual sensitivity and mindfulness meditation.' Perceptual and Motor Skills 1984;58:775-84.

17 Coehlo R., Silva C., Maia A. et al. Bone mineral density and depression: a community study in women. J of Psychosomatic Research 1999;46(1):29-35.

18 Kabat-Zinn J. et al. Four year follow-up of a meditation based program for the self-regulation of chronic pain; treatment outcomes and compliance. Clinical Journal of Pain 1987;2:159-73.

19 Wilson A. et al. Transcendental meditation and asthma. Respiration 1975;32:74-80.

20 Cerpa H. 'The effects of clinically standardised meditation on type 2 diabetics.' Dissertation Abstracts International 1989;499(8b): 3432.

21 Kabat-Zinn J. et al. Effectiveness of a meditation based stress reduction program in the treatment of anxiety disorders. Am J Psychiatry 1992;149:936-43.

22 Eppley K. et al. 'Differential effects of relaxation techniques on trait anxiety: a meta-analysis.' Journal of Clinical Psychology 1989; 45(6):957-74.

23 Teasdale J., Segal Z., Williams J. How does cognitive therapy prevent depressive relapse and why should attention control (mindfulness) training help? Behaviour Research and Therapy. 1995;33(1):25-39.

24 Bujatti M., Riederer P. Serotonin, noradrenaline, dopamine metabolites in TM technique. J of Neural Transmission. 1976;39(3):257-67.

25 Alexander C. et al. 'TM, self-actualisation, and psychological health: a conceptual overview and statistical meta-analysis.' Journal of Social Behaviour and Personality 1991;6(5):189-248.

26 Kornfield J. 'Intensive insight meditation: a phenomenonological study.' Journal of Transpersonal Psychology 1979;11(1):48-51.

27 Kutz I., Lerserman J. Dorrington C. et al. Meditation as an adjunct to psychotherapy. An outcome study. Psychotherapy and Psychosomatics 1985;43(4):209-18.

28 Gelderloos P. et al. Effectiveness of the TM program in preventing and treating substance misuse: a review. Int J Addict 1991;26:293-325.

29 Mason L., Alexander C., Travis F. et al. Electrophysiological correlates of higher states of consciousness during sleep in long-term practitioners of the TM program. Sleep 1997;20(2):102-10.

30 Abrams A. et al. 'The TM program and rehabilitation at Folsom Prison: a cross-validation study.' Criminal Justice and Behaviour 1978;5(1):3-20.

31 Carrington P., Collings G., Benson H. et al. The use of meditation and relaxation techniques for the management of stress in a working population. J of Occupational Medicine 1980;22(4):221-31.

32 Fiebert M. et al. 'Meditation and academic performance.' Perceptual and Motor Skills 1981;53(2):447-50.

33 Verma I. et al. 'Effect of TM on the performance of some cognitive and psychological tests.' International Journal of Medical Research 1982;7:136-43.

34 Delmonte M. et al. 'Conceptual models and functions of meditation in psychotherapy.' Journal of Contemporary Psychotherapy 1987; 17(1):38-59.

35 Lucassen P., Assendelft W., Gubbels J. et al. Effectiveness of treatment for infantile colic: a systematic review. BMJ 1998;316(7144): 1563-9.

36 Hassed C. Meditation in general practice. Australian Family Physician August 1996;25(8):1257-60.

37 Astin J. Stress reduction through mindfulness meditation. Effects on psychological symptomatology, sense of control, and spiritual experiences. Psychotherapy and Psychosomatics 1997;66(2):97-106.

38 Shapiro S., Schwartz G., Bonner G. Effects of mindfulness-based stress reduction on medical and pre-medical students. J Behav Med 1998;21(6):581-99.

39 Kabat-Zinn et al. Effectiveness of meditation based stress reduction program in the treatment of anxiety disorders. Am J Psychiatry 1992;149:936-943.

40 Teasdale J, Segal Z, Williams J, Mark G. How does cognitive therapy prevent depressive relapse and why should attention control (mindfulness) training help? Behav Res Ther 1995;33:25-39.

41 Teasdale J, Segal Z, Williams J et al. Prevention of relapse/recurrence in major depression by mindfulness-based gognitive therapy. J Consul Clin Psychol 2000;68(4):615-23.

42 Speca M, Carlson L, Goodey E, Angen M. A randomised wait-list controlled trial: the effects of a mindfulness meditation based stress reduction program on kood and symptoms of stress in cancer patients. Psychosomatic Medicine 2000;62:613-22.

43 Kaplan K, Goldenberg D, Galvin-Nadeau M. The impact of a meditation-based stress reduction program on fibromyalgia. Gen Hosp Psychiatry 1993;15:284-9.

44 Kabat-Zinn J. et al. Four-year follow-up of a meditation based program for the self-regulation of chronic pain: treatment outcomes and compliance. Clin J Pain 1987;2159-173.

45 Kristeller J, Hallett C. An exploratory study of a meditation-based intervention for binge eating disorder. J Health Psychol 1999;4:357-63.

46 Wenneberg SR, Schneider RH, Walton KG et al. A controlled study of the effects of the Transcendental Meditation program on cardio-vascular reactivity and ambulatory blood pressure. Int J Neurosci 1997;89:15-28.

47 Castillo-Richmond A, Schneider R, Alexander C et al. Effects of stress reduction on carotid atherosclerosis in hypertensive African Americans. Stroke 2000;31:568-73.

48 Nagarathna R. et al. Yoga for bronchial asthma: a controlled study. BMJ 1985;291:1077-1079

49 Ornish D. et al. Can lifestyle changes severse coronary heart disease? Lancet 1990;336:129-133.